Open doors

Student's Book 1

NORMAN
WHITNEY

OXFORD UNIVERSITY PRESS 1994

CONTENTS

	a		b		c		d	
	Presentation	**Communication Pronunciation**	**Grammar**	**Study skills**	**Vocabulary**	**English across the curriculum**	**Skills work**	**Progress diary Song**
1	*No disco for you!*	Numbers *1–20* Greetings, names and ages *Hello! What's your name? How old are you?* The sounds /iː/ /ɪ/	Present simple of *be* (affirmative) Personal pronouns *I, you …* Articles *the, a/an*	The English alphabet *How do you spell …?*	Days of the week/ Months of the year Numbers *1st–12th* **Learn this!** *on/in*	School subjects and timetables	Personal details and interests	***Progress diary 1*** ♫ *The seven days a week blues*
2	*Where are you from?*	Numbers *20–100* Greetings *Good morning …* *Where's Maria from?* The sounds /ɑː/ /æ/	Present simple of *be* (negative and interrogative) Demonstrative pronouns *this/that/these/those*	Capital letters **Learn this!** Plural forms	In the classroom *chair, table …* **Learn this!** *There is/are …*	Geography: the British Isles **Learn this!** *in/at/on*	Letters and cassettes to penfriends (1)	***Progress diary 2*** ♫ *We are the champions!*
3	*Nick's family*	Introducing people *This is … Pleased to meet you.* Talking about families *Who's this? He's my brother.* The sounds /uː/ /ʊ/	Present simple of regular verbs (affirmative) Possessive adjectives *my, your …* Plural forms **Learn this!** Possessive forms	*What's the English word for …?*	Members of the family *mother, father …* **Learn this!** Demonstrative adjectives *this/ that/these/those*	International studies: countries and nationalities	Letters and cassettes to penfriends (2) **Learn this!** *and/but*	***Progress diary 3*** ♫ *All around the world*
4	*Do you eat octopus?*	Likes and dislikes *I like … I don't like … Do you like …?* Offering, accepting and refusing *Would you like a …?* The sounds /ɔː/ /ɒ/	Present simple of regular verbs (negative and interrogative) Countable and uncountable nouns *some* and *any*	Learning new words	Food and drink *potatoes, tea …*	Mathematics: + − x ÷	School meals Prices	***Progress diary 4*** ♫ *One, two, one, two, three!*
5	*No, you can't!*	*What's the time? It's five past nine. What time does …?* Talking about permission *At home I can …, but I can't …* The sounds /ɜː/ /e/	Revision of present simple The verb *can*	Memorizing Asking and answering about dates	Houses and homes *hall, living-room, kitchen …* **Learn this!** *in/on*	Cross cultural studies: houses and homes around the world	Where people live Dream homes	***Progress diary 5*** ♫ *Gordon the Ghost!*
6	*Sports clothes*	Instructions *Be careful! Don't be late!* Talking about possession *Have you got …?* The sounds /ʌ/ /æ/	The verb *have got* Imperatives The pronoun *one/ones*	Using vocabulary topics	Clothes *sweater, shoes, skirt …* **Learn this!** *a pair of …*	Natural science: animals in danger	Pets	***Progress diary 6*** ♫ *Fashion Queen!*

1a NO DISCO FOR YOU!

🎧 1

1 Nick and Gary are on a number six bus.

Nick Fifty pence, please.
Woman How old are you?
Nick I'm fifteen. He's fourteen.
Woman You're an adult! One pound, please.
Nick Oh, OK.

2 Sara and Tina are outside the disco.

Man How old are you?
Sara I'm fourteen. She's fifteen.
Man No disco for you!

3 **Nick** Hello!
Sara Hi!
Nick I'm Nick. What's your name?
Sara Sara.

4 **Gary** Look!
Tina Brilliant!

Comprehension

1 Answer the questions in your notebook.

How old is Nick?

Fifteen.

1 How old is Gary? ......
2 How old is Sara? ......
3 How old is Tina? ......

2 Write the names.

I'm fifteen.

Nick.

1 **He**'s fourteen. ......
2 **She**'s fifteen. ......
3 **I**'m fourteen. ......
4 **They**'re on a bus. ...... and ......

Numbers

3 Listen and repeat. 2

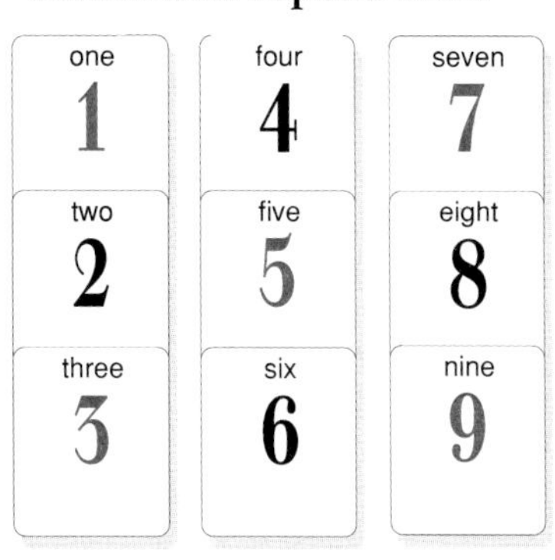

Look and say. *It's the number one bus.*

4 Listen and repeat. 3

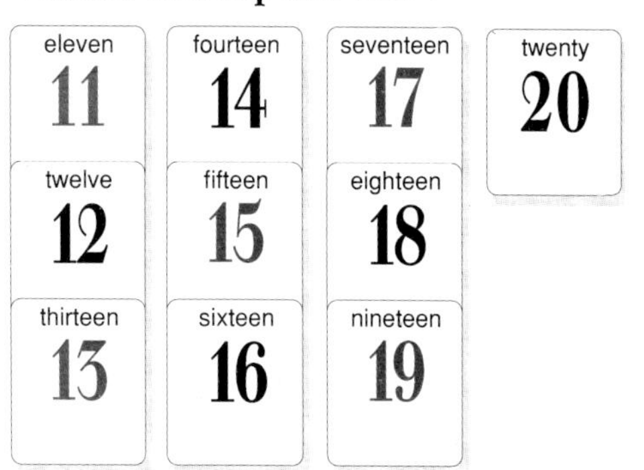

Look and say. *She's thirteen years old.*

Communication

Greetings, names and ages

5 Listen and repeat. 4

Sara Hello. What's your name?
Nick Hi. My name's Nick.
Sara How old are you, Nick?
Nick I'm fifteen.

Now ask and answer with a partner.

You Hello. What's your name?
Partner Hi. My name's ......
You How old are you?
Partner I'm ......

Pronunciation

6 Listen and repeat. 5

long /iː/	short /ɪ/
three	six
Tina	Nick

Listen, repeat and write. Is each sound long or short?

1 he 2 disco 3 brilliant 4 she

1b Grammar

The verb *be*: present simple tense (affirmative)

1 **Compare the full and short forms of the verb *be*.**

2 **Write the sentences in your notebook. Use *'s, 're, 'm*.**

Hello. My name ...... Sue.

Hello. My name's Sue.

1 I ...... a teenager.

2 Mike ...... my friend.

3 He ...... sixteen years old.

4 We ...... students.

5 No, Mike! You ...... an adult.

3 **Complete Mike's letter. Use *are, is, am*.**

17 Croft Road
London

Dear Mr Jones,

My name (1) ...... Mike Smith and I (2) ...... sixteen years old. My friend Sue (3) ...... seventeen years old. We (4) .... students. As you (5) ...... the manager of Hamburger House and...

Personal pronouns

4 **Copy and complete the chart with the correct personal pronouns. Use *he, we, you, I, they, it, she*.**

	personal pronouns (subject) *singular*	*plural*
1st person	I	we
2nd person	you	_ _ _
3rd person (woman)	_ _	_ _ _ _
(man)	_ _ _	_ _ _ _
(telephone)	_ _	_ _ _ _

5 **Write the sentences with the correct personal pronoun.**

What's my name? ......'s Mike.

What's my name? It's Mike.

1 ......'m a teenager.

2 How old is Sara? ......'s fourteen.

3 Sue and I are students. ......'re friends.

4 Sue, how old are ......?

English articles

6 Learn the English articles.

definite article: **the**	<u>**The**</u> Pizza Palace.
indefinite article: **a/an**	Nick is <u>**a**</u> student.
	She is <u>**an**</u> adult.

What's the difference? Write *a* or *an*.

1 It's ...... pizza.

2 It's ...... orange.

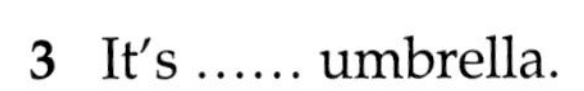

3 It's ...... umbrella.

4 It's ...... table.

Study skills

The English alphabet

7 Copy and complete the letters of the English alphabet in your notebook.

8 Do the alphabet rap! 6

Spelling

9 Listen and repeat. 7

Gary How do you spell 'Nick'?
Nick Nick? N – I – C – K.
Tina How do you spell 'pizza'?
Sara Pizza? P – I – double Z – A.

Now ask and answer about spelling.

1

2

You choose!

1c Vocabulary

Days of the week

1 Listen and repeat. 🎧 8

Monday
Tuesday
Wednesday
Thursday
Friday
Saturday
Sunday

2 Here are this week's special offers. Write them in the correct order in your notebook.

Monday Free chocolate ice-cream
Tuesday ......

Months of the year

3 Listen and repeat. 🎧 9

January
February
March
April
May
June
July
August
September
October
November
December

Numbers

4 Listen and repeat. 🎧 10

first
second
third
fourth
fifth
sixth
seventh
eighth
ninth
tenth
eleventh
twelfth

Now write the words and the numbers in the correct order.

first 1st
second ......

5 Complete the sentences. Use months and numbers.

March is the third month of the year.

1 December is the ...... month of the year.
2 May is the ...... month of the year.
3 June is the ...... month of the year.
4 ...... is the tenth month of the year.
5 ...... is the eighth month of the year.
6 ...... is the second month of the year.

Learn this!
The disco is <u>on</u> Saturday.
The disco is <u>on</u> 1 October.
The disco is <u>in</u> October.

English across the curriculum

School subjects and timetables

1 **Look at the pictures of school subjects in the timetable. Match the pictures with these words.**

Art	History
Cookery	Library/Private study
Computer studies	Maths
English	Music
French	Science
Geography	Sports

3 **Ask and answer about school.**

You What's the third lesson on Monday?

Partner The third lesson on Monday is Science.

You What's the first lesson on ......?

Partner The first lesson on ......

ST GEORGE'S COMPREHENSIVE SCHOOL
Timetable for Year 9 Class A

	Lesson									
Day	1	2		3	4		5		6	7
Monday			B R			L U		B R		
Tuesday			E			N		E		
Wednesday			A K			C H		A K		

2 **Copy and complete the timetable in your notebook. Write the correct words.**

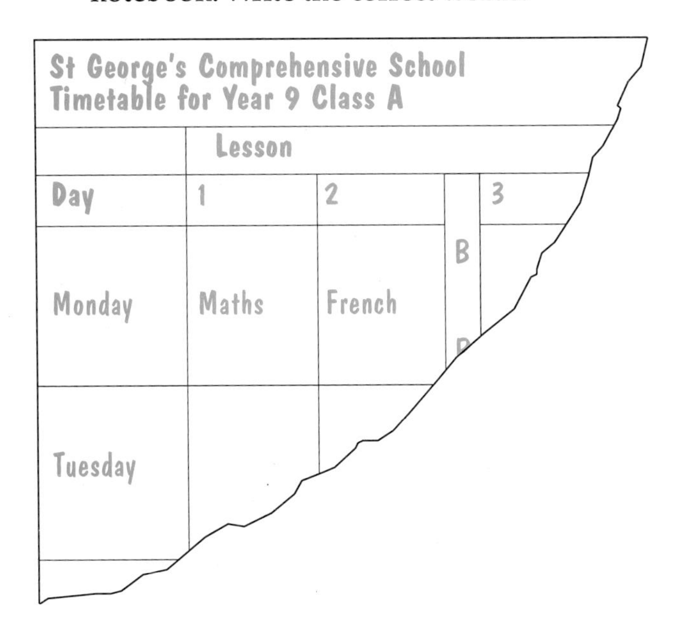

St George's Comprehensive School
Timetable for Year 9 Class A

	Lesson			
Day	1	2		3
Monday	Maths	French	B	
Tuesday				

1d Skills work

Reading

1 **Read about Stephen and answer the questions in your notebook.**

Stephen is fifteen years old. He is in year 11.
His favourite subject is History and his favourite sport is football.

1 What is the student's name? *Stephen.*
2 How old is he?
3 What year is he in?
4 What is his favourite subject?
5 What is his favourite sport?

Listening

2 **Listen to Gloria and Philip. Complete the notes.** 11

football

ice hockey

tennis

swimming

baseball

gymnastics

athletics

Name	*Gloria*	*Philip*
Age		
Year at school		
Favourite subject		
Favourite sport		

Speaking

3 **Interview a friend in your class. Ask and answer about name, age, favourite subjects and favourite sports.**

Writing

4 **Now write about your friend.**

My friend's name is …… .
She/He is …… years old.
She/He is in the …… year at school.
Her/His favourite subject is …… .
Her/His favourite sport is …… .

Progress Diary 1

Grammar

1 Complete the table in your notebook.
The verb *be*

full forms	*short forms*
I am	I'm
you are	......

2 Complete the list.
Personal pronouns

singular I, you, ...	*plural* we, ...

3 Write *a* or *an*.

...... disco	...... bus	...... orange
...... apple	...... girl	...... pizza

Vocabulary

4 Complete the lists.

one, two, ... twenty.
first, second, ... twelfth.
Monday, ...
January, ...

Communication

5 Write a conversation between John and Kate.

name?	**John**	What's ......?
	Kate	My ....
age?	**John**	How ......?
	Kate	I'm ....
favourite subject?	**Kate**	What's ......?
	John	My ....
favourite sport?	**Kate**	What's ......?
	John	My ....

Pronunciation

6 Complete the table. Use *disco, six, we, three.*

long /iː/	**short /ɪ/**
we	......
......	......

My progress

not good OK good

In unit 1	I like	I don't like ......

The seven days a week blues

Listen and complete the words of the song. 12

(1) ...... blue
(2) ...... too
(3) ......, (4) ......, (5) ......, baby
I love you

(6) ...... night
(7) ...... too
Seven days a week, baby
I love you

2a WHERE ARE YOU FROM?

 1

1 There are two students in the Pizza Palace.

Nick Hi! My name's Nick.
Ana Hello! I'm Ana and this is Petros.
Nick Where are you from, Ana?
Ana I'm from Spain.
Nick Are you from Spain, Petros?
Petros No, I'm not. I'm from Greece.
Nick Are you students here in London?
Ana Yes, we are.

2 **Waitress** Good evening!
All Hi!
Sara Hey, these pizzas aren't cheap! They're expensive!
Waitress No, they aren't. Look! That's the special menu today.

3 **Tina** Ugh! This pizza is horrible!
Gary No, it isn't. It's great!

4 **Gary** Bye, Tina. This is my phone number.
Tina Oh, thanks, Gary.
Nick Bye, Sara!
Sara Goodbye, Nick.

Comprehension

1 True or false?

Nick is from England.

True.

Ana is from England.

False. Ana is from Spain.

1 Petros is from Greece.
2 Gary isn't from Spain.
3 Gary and Tina are from Spain.
4 Sara and Nick aren't from England.
5 Petros: 'I'm from Greece.'
6 Ana: 'I'm not from Spain.'

Numbers

2 Listen and repeat. 2

20	twenty	50	fifty	80	eighty
30	thirty	60	sixty	90	ninety
40	forty	70	seventy	100	a hundred

3 Listen and repeat. 3

21	twenty-one	65	sixty-five
32	thirty-two	76	seventy-six
43	forty-three	87	eighty-seven
54	fifty-four	98	ninety-eight

Write the words.

26 = twenty-six 42 = ……

35 = …… 58 = ……

Write the numbers.

sixty-one = 61 eighty-three = ……

seventy-eight = …… ninety-four = ……

Communication

Greetings

4 Listen and repeat. 4

Good morning! Good afternoon!

Good evening! Goodnight!

Hello! Hi! Goodbye! Bye!

5 Listen and repeat. Then ask and answer about the other people. 5

Nick Where's Maria from?

Ana She's from Portugal.

Nick Where are Patrick and Kate from?

Ana They're from Ireland.

Pronunciation

6 Listen and repeat. 6

long /ɑː/	short /æ/
are	that
large	thanks

Listen, repeat and write. Is each sound long or short?

1 man 2 aren't 3 Art 4 Maths

2b Grammar

The verb *be*: present simple tense (negative and interrogative)

1 **Compare the full forms and the short forms of the negative of the verb *be*.**

full forms	*short forms*
I **am not**	I'**m not**
you **are not**	you **aren't**
she / he / it **is not**	she / he / it **isn't**
we / you / they **are not**	we / you / they **aren't**

2 **Complete the sentences in your notebook. Use *'m not, aren't, isn't*.**

Linda ...... from England, she's from Ireland.

Linda isn't from England, she's from Ireland.

1 Ana ...... from England, she's from Spain.
2 Lydia: 'I ...... from Italy, I'm from Poland.'
3 Gary: 'You ...... from England, you're from America.'
4 Elena and Paulo ...... from Portugal, they're from Brazil.
5 Petros ...... from Ireland, he's from Greece.
6 Sara's from England, she ...... from Australia.

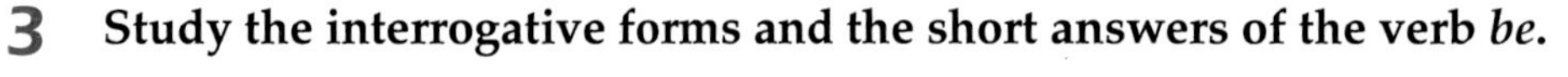

3 **Study the interrogative forms and the short answers of the verb *be*.**

interrogative	*answers*	
Am I ...?	Yes, I **am**.	No, I'**m not**.
Are you ...?	Yes, you **are**.	No, you **aren't**.
Is she / he / it ...?	Yes, she / he / it **is**.	No, she / he / it **isn't**.
Are we / you / they ...?	Yes, we / you / they **are**.	No, we / you / they **aren't**.

4 **Complete the questions. Then give true answers.**

...... you at home?

Q *Are you at home?*

A *Yes, I am.* **or** *No, I'm not.*

1 ...... you at school?

2 ...... your friends at school today?

3 ...... Nick fifteen?

4 ...... Linda from Scotland?

5 ...... your English teacher at home today?

5 **Rewrite the dialogue in the correct order.**

Hi, Linda. I'm Darren. Where are you from?

I'm fourteen. Are you fourteen, too?

No, I'm not. I'm from England.

Hi. My name's Linda.

How old are you, Darren?

Yes, I am.

I'm from Ireland. Are you?

Demonstrative pronouns

6 **Write the sentences. Use *this, that, these, those.***

This is an apple.

Those are buses.

Learn this!

singular	plural
one boy	two boys
one girl	two girls
one orange	two oranges
one pizza	two pizzas

Study skills

Capital letters

7 **Learn the rules for capital letters.**

The first word in a sentence

He's fourteen. **T**hey're adults.

Names

Sara **G**ary

Days of the week

Tuesday **S**unday

Months of the year

May **D**ecember

Countries

England **G**reece

Nationalities

English **G**reek

School subjects

History **G**eography

The personal pronoun 'I'

Hi! **I**'m Mike.

8 **Write the sentences with the correct capital letters.**

sara and tina are friends.

Sara and Tina are friends.

1 sara, nick and gary are students.

2 it's monday, september the tenth.

3 the first lesson is maths.

4 his favourite subject is science.

5 it's expensive!

6 ana is from spain.

2c

Vocabulary

In the classroom

1 Listen and repeat. 🎧 7

2 Look at the picture above. Listen and repeat. 🎧 8

There's a blackboard in the classroom.

There isn't a computer on the table.

There are four chairs.

There aren't three doors.

True or false?

There's a man in the classroom.

True.

1 There's a girl in the classroom.

2 There's a window.

3 There are two doors.

4 There isn't a woman.

5 There aren't two tables.

6 There aren't four chairs.

3 Look at one picture. Ask and answer.

You Is there ...... in your picture?

Partner Yes, there is. / No, there isn't.

You Are there ...... in your picture?

Partner Yes, there are. / No, there aren't.

Learn this!

singular	plural
There's ...	There are ...
There isn't ...	There aren't ...
Is there ...?	Are there ...?

English across the curriculum

Geography

1 **Listen *carefully* to the geography lesson. Complete the information in your notebook.** 🎧 **9**

1. There are **three** countries in 'Great Britain'. They are ……
2. There are **four** countries in 'The United Kingdom'. They are ……

2 **Where are the cities? Ask and answer with a partner.**

You Where's London?

Partner London? It's in the south-east of England.

Manchester   Cork   *You choose!*

3 **Draw a map of your country, with towns and cities. Then ask and answer about their locations.**

Learn this!

<u>in</u> England	<u>at</u> home	<u>on</u> the table
<u>in</u> the south	<u>at</u> school	<u>on</u> the desk

2d Skills work

Reading

1 **Read Helen's letter to her penfriend, Juan, in Spain.**

2 **Copy and complete the notes about Helen in your notebook.**

1 First name Helen
2 Family name Jones
3 Town ......
4 Country ......
5 Age ......
6 Name of school ......
7 Year ......
8 Number in the class ......
9 Favourite singer ......

22 Newport Road
Cardiff
CF6 4TU
Wales

16 October

Dear Juan,

Hello! I'm your new penfriend. My name is Helen. That's my first name. My family name is Jones.

I'm from Cardiff, in Wales. I'm fifteen years old. The name of my school is the Central Cardiff Comprehensive. I am in Year 10. There are twenty-seven students in my class.

My favourite singer is Prince. Who is your favourite?

Best wishes,

Helen

This is a photo of me!

Listening

3 **Thanos lives in Greece. Anne lives in Scotland. Listen to Thanos' cassette letter. Which is the picture of Thanos and his family?** 10

Speaking

4 **Imagine you are from Britain. Answer these questions about yourself.**

1 What's your first name?

My first name's ...

2 What's your family name?
3 What town and country are you from?
4 How old are you?
5 What's the name of your school?
6 Which year are you in?
7 How many are there in your class?
8 Who's your favourite singer?

Now interview two other students.

PROGRESS DIARY 2

Grammar

1 Complete the table in your notebook.

The verb *be*		
I am/I'm	I am not/I'm not	Am I ...?
you are/you're	......	......
she is/she's	......	......

2 Translate.

This is ...	That is ...	
These are ...	Those are ...	
There is ...	There isn't ...	Is there ...?
There are ...	There aren't ...	Are there ...?

Vocabulary

3 Name five things in your classroom.

window, ...

Communication

4 Here are the answers. Write the questions.

Q ...... **A** She's from England.

Q ...... **A** No, he isn't from Spain. He's from Greece.

5 What's the greeting?

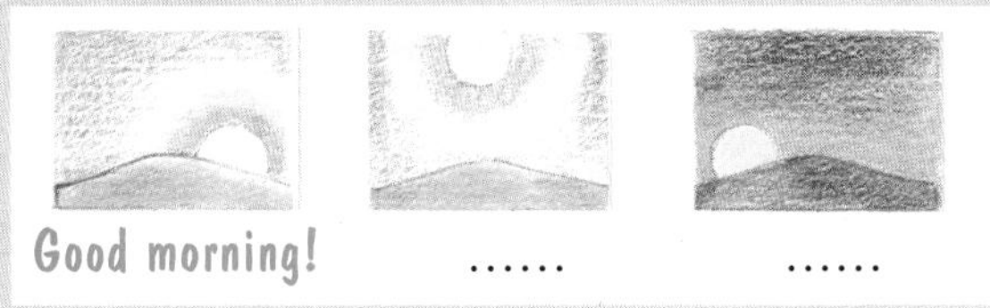

Good morning! ....

Pronunciation

6 Complete the table. Use *Art, Maths, Cardiff, map*.

long /ɑː/	short /æ/
Art	......
......	......

My progress

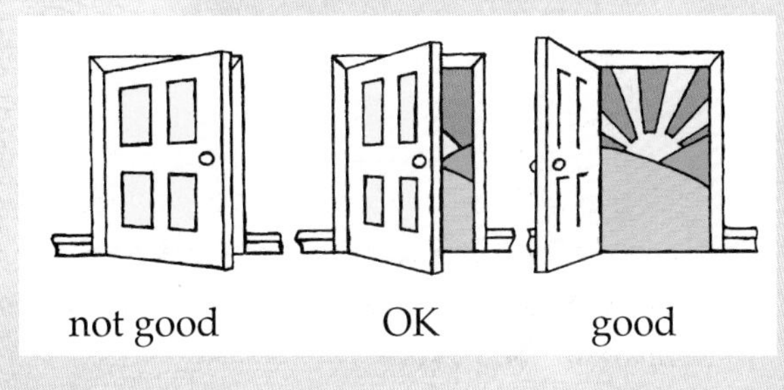

not good OK good

In unit 2 I like ...... I don't like ......

We are the champions!

Listen and complete the words of the song. 11

We are the champions!
Two, **(1)** ......, **(2)** ......, **(3)** ......
Our team is great!

We are the champions!
North, **(4)** ...... , **(5)** ......
and **(6)** ......
Our team is the best!

3a NICK'S FAMILY

1

(1)

Nick Johnson lives with his parents, and his sister. They live in Wembley, in north London. Nick's mum is called Sue. She works in a supermarket. His dad is called Jim and he works in a bank. Nick's sister is called Tracy. She is nine years old. There is also a dog in the family. His name is Fred.

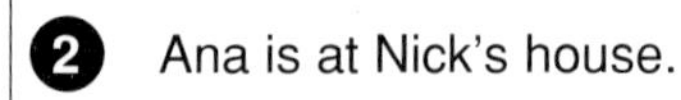

(2) Ana is at Nick's house.

Nick Ana, this is my mum.
Ana Hello, Mrs Johnson. Pleased to meet you.
Nick Oh, and this is our dog. He's called Fred! He likes visitors!

(3)

Nick These are my grandparents.
Ana Are they your mum's parents?
Nick Yes. They're called Mr and Mrs Macintosh. They live in Scotland.

(4) **Ana** Who's this?
Nick Oh, that's Tracy, my little sister. And this is our cousin. He's called Tony.
Tracy Hello! Who are you? Are you Nick's new girlfriend?
Nick Oh, Tracy! I hate you!

Comprehension

1 **Who are they? Write the answers in your notebook. Choose from *Nick's cousin, Nick's mum, Nick's dad, Nick's dog, Nick's grandparents, Nick's sister.***

Who is Sue Johnson?

Nick's mum.

1 **Who** is Tracy? ......
2 **Who** is Tony? ......
3 **Who** are Mr and Mrs Macintosh? ......
4 **Who** is Jim Johnson? ......
5 **Who** is Fred? ......

2 **Who are they? Write the answers. Choose from *Fred, Mr and Mrs Macintosh, Mr Johnson, Mrs Johnson, Nick, The Johnson family.***

He works in a bank.

Mr Johnson.

1 **She** works in a supermarket.
2 **He** likes visitors. ......
3 **He** hates his sister! ......
4 **They** live in Scotland. ......
5 **They** live in London. ......

Communication

Introducing people

3 **Listen and repeat.** 2

Nick Ana, this is my mum.

Ana Hello, Mrs Johnson. Pleased to meet you.

Nick Mum, this is Ana.

Mrs Johnson Hello, Ana. Nice to meet you.

Now introduce two people to each other. Use English names!

Talking about families

4 **Listen and repeat the dialogue between Tracy and her new friend Tom.** 3

Tom Who's this, Tracy?

Tracy He's my brother. He's called Nick.

Tom Who's that?

Tracy She's my mum. She's called Sue.

Tom Who are they?

Tracy They're my grandparents. They're called Mr and Mrs Macintosh.

5 **Use photos of your families. Ask and answer about the people in the photos.**

You Who's this?

Partner He's my ... He's called ...

You Who are they?

Partner They're my ... They're called ...

Pronunciation

6 **Listen and repeat.** 4

long /uː/	short /ʊ/
you	look
who	good

Listen, repeat and write. Is each sound long or short?

1 two   2 book

3 whose   4 cook

3b Grammar

Present simple tense (affirmative)

1 Study the table of regular verbs.

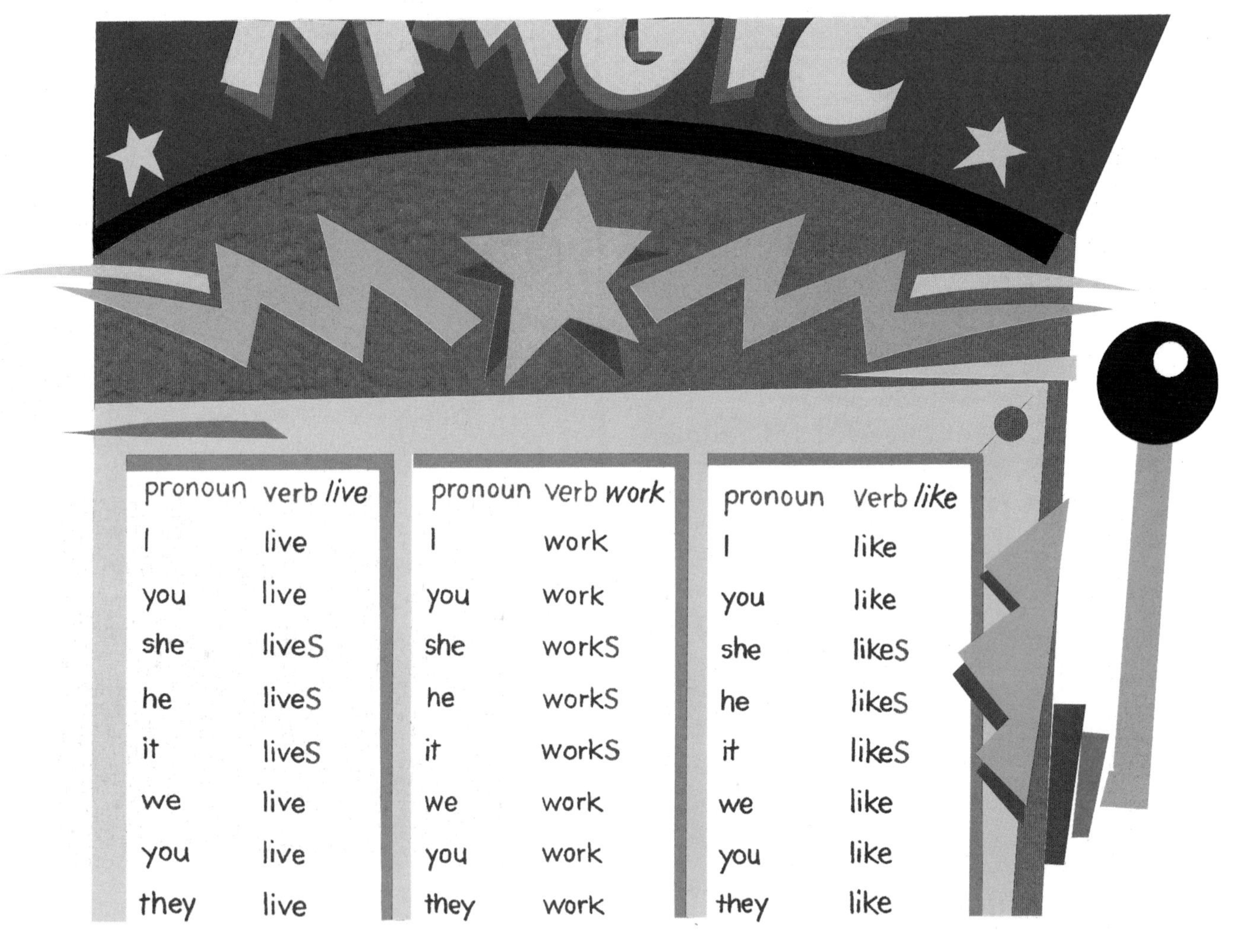

pronoun	verb *live*	pronoun	verb *work*	pronoun	verb *like*
I	live	I	work	I	like
you	live	you	work	you	like
she	liveS	she	workS	she	likeS
he	liveS	he	workS	he	likeS
it	liveS	it	workS	it	likeS
we	live	we	work	we	like
you	live	you	work	you	like
they	live	they	work	they	like

2 Write the sentences in your notebook. Use the correct form of each verb.

She ...... in England. (live)
She lives in England.

1 He ...... in Scotland. (live)
2 We ...... dancing. (like)
3 They ...... in a supermarket. (work)
4 You ...... with your family. (live)
5 I ...... London. (like)
6 Sue's mum ...... in London. (work)
7 Mike ...... discos. (like)
8 Sue's cousins ...... in north London. (live)
9 Mike's sister ...... dancing. (like)
10 Nick ...... Tracy! (hate)

Possessive adjectives

3 Copy and complete the chart with the correct possessive adjectives. Use *his, our, its, your, their, my, her.*

	personal pronouns (subject)	possessive adjectives
singular	I	my
	you	......
	she	......
	he	......
	it	......

	personal pronouns (subject)	possessive adjectives
plural	we	......
	you	......
	they	......

4 Write each sentence with the correct possessive adjective.

You live with ...... sister.

You live with your sister.

1 **She** likes ...... English teacher.
2 **They** live with ...... father.
3 **He** works in ...... father's shop.
4 **I** live with ...... grandparents.
5 **Linda** likes dancing with ...... friends.
6 Hello, **I'm** Mrs Jackson. Darren is ...... son.
7 Hi, **Linda**! Is this ...... cassette?
8 **Mr and Mrs Jackson** live with ...... two children.

Singular and plural

5 Compare the singular and plural forms.

regular nouns			
group 1		**group 2**	
singular	*plural*	*singular*	*plural*
book	books	bus	buses
map	maps	sandwich	sandwiches
girl	girls		
boy	boys		

demonstrative pronouns	
singular	*plural*
this is	these are
that is	those are

articles	
singular	*plural*
a book	books
an apple	apples
the book	the books
the apple	the apples

6 Change the sentences:

from singular to plural.

That's a book.

Those are books.

1 This is a desk.
2 This is an apple.
3 That is a pen.
4 That isn't an orange.

from plural to singular.

Those aren't pizzas.

That isn't a pizza.

5 These aren't rulers.
6 Those are apples.
7 These are students.
8 Those aren't teachers.

Whose ...?

7 Ask and answer about possession.

You Whose book is this?

Partner It's Sue's.

You choose!

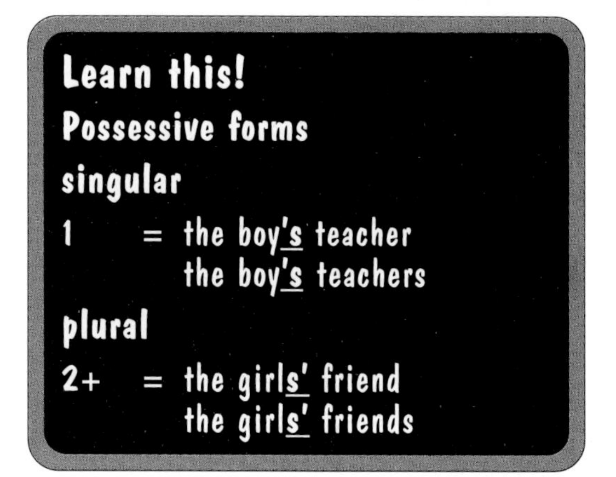

Study skills

What's the English word for ...?

8 Ask and answer about words in English.

You What's the English word for ...?

Partner Book.

You choose!

3c Vocabulary

Members of the family

1 **Listen and repeat.** 5

1 parents
2 mother
3 father
4 children
5 daughter
6 son
7 sister
8 brother
9 grandparents
10 grandmother
11 grandfather
12 grandchildren
13 granddaughter
14 grandson
15 aunt
16 uncle
17 cousin

2 **Don is thirteen years old and lives in London.**
Listen to Don and complete his family tree in your notebook. 6

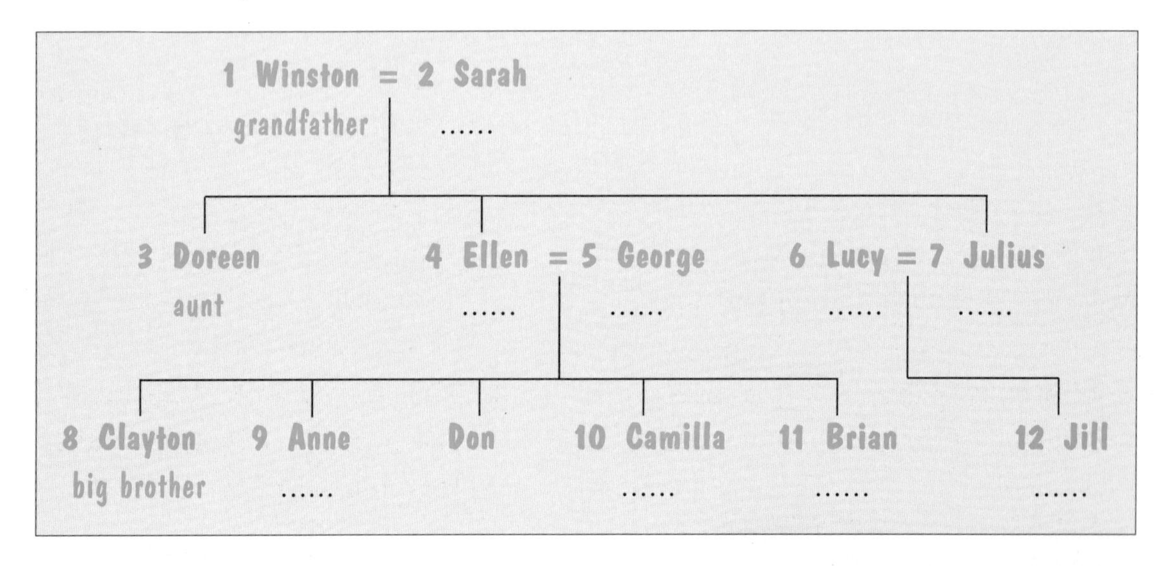

3 **Imagine your partner is Don. Ask and answer.**

You Who's this boy, Don?
Partner/Don That's my brother.
You What's his name?
Partner/Don His name is Brian.

Learn this!
Demonstrative adjectives

This boy	That girl
These boy**s**	Those girl**s**

English across the curriculum

International studies: countries and nationalities

1 Study the world map. Listen and repeat the names of the countries. 7

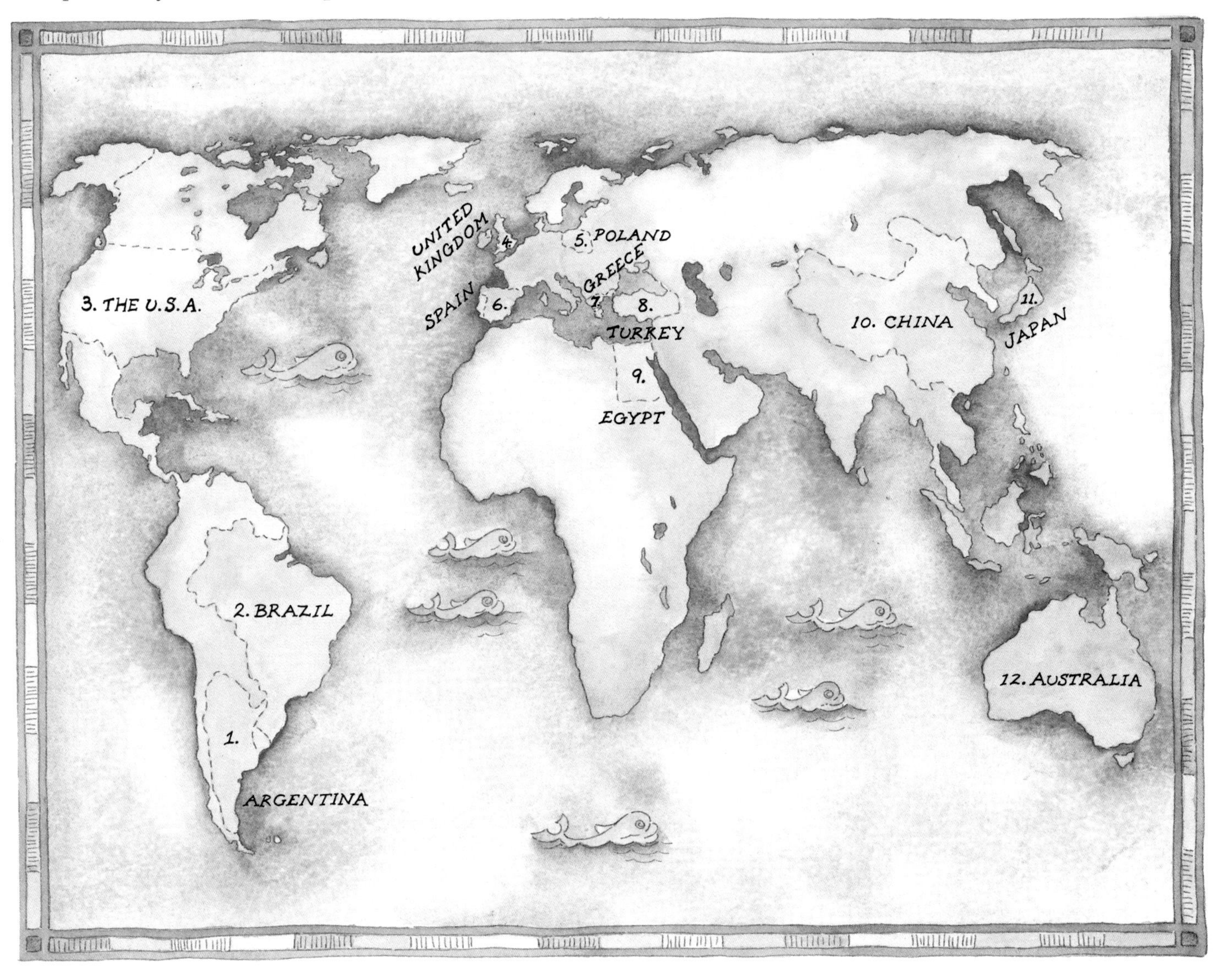

2 Match the countries and the nationalities. Use:

British	Polish	Greek
Australian	Turkish	Brazilian
American	Spanish	Japanese
Argentinian	Chinese	Egyptian

	Countries	Nationalities
1	Argentina	Argentinian
2	Brazil	

Now listen and check your answers. 8

3 Complete the sentences.

She's from Spain. She's ......

She's from Spain. She's Spanish.

1 I'm from Japan. I'm ......

2 We're from Greece. We're ......

3 They're from the United Kingdom. They're ......

4 He's from Brazil. He's ......

He's Australian. He's from ......

He's Australian. He's from Australia.

5 You're Argentinian. You're from ......

6 He's Turkish. He's from ......

7 We're Polish. We're from ......

8 I'm Egyptian. I'm from ......

3d Skills work

Reading

1 **Juan lives in Spain. Helen lives in Wales. Read Juan's letter to Helen.**

C/ García de Cortázar 30, 2º – B
Oviedo
10 November

Dear Helen,

Hello! Thank you for your letter.

I'm fourteen years old and I'm in the second year at secondary school. We study English on Monday, Wednesday and Thursday.

My dad works in a hotel and my mum works in a hospital. My sister is sixteen years old and her name is Isabel. My little brother is called José Martín. He is only seven.

I like jazz, but my favourite music is pop music. My favourite singer is Martika. She is Spanish.

My favourite subject at school is Geography and my favourite sport is volleyball, but I also play football.

I enclose a postcard of Oviedo, and a photo of my family.

Best wishes,

Juan

Writing

2 **Correct these false statements about Juan. Write the answers in your notebook.**

Juan is fifteen years old.

He is fourteen years old.

1 He lives in Barcelona.
2 He studies English on Tuesday and Friday.
3 Juan's mum works in a hotel.
4 His sister is called Maria.
5 His brother is sixteen years old.
6 His favourite music is jazz.
7 His favourite singer is American.
8 His favourite subject is History.

Listening

3 **Anne lives in Scotland. Thanos lives in Greece. Listen to Anne's cassette letter to Thanos. Choose the correct answers.** 9

1 The date of Anne's letter is
  a) Sunday 2 November
  b) Monday 2 November
  c) Monday 2 September
2 Anne is
  a) fourteen years old
  b) fifteen years old
  c) sixteen years old
3 She lives with
  a) her mother
  b) her father
  c) her mother and her father
4 She lives with
  a) her brother and sister
  b) her two brothers and one sister
  c) her two sisters and one brother
5 She plays
  a) tennis
  b) basketball
  c) American football
6 Her favourite music is
  a) pop
  b) classical
  c) jazz

Learn this!

Conjunctions

Spain **and** Greece are in Europe.

Canada is in North America, **but** Brazil is in South America.

Progress Diary 3

Grammar

1 Complete the tables in your notebook.

Present simple tense (affirmative)

I like   we ......
you like
she likes
he ......

Possessive adjectives

I	my
you	......
she	......
......	

2 How do you say these in your language?

This boy   **That** girl
These men   **Those** women

Vocabulary

3 Write as many words as you can about the family.

male	*female*	*male <u>or</u> female*
son	daughter	child/children
father	......	......
......	......	

4 Write the names of five countries and nationalities.

Australia – Australian, ...

Communication

5 How do you say these in your language?

This is ......
Nice to meet you.
Pleased to meet you.

Pronunciation

6 Complete the table. Use *book, music, whose, good*.

long /uː/	short /ʊ/
whose	......
......	......

My progress

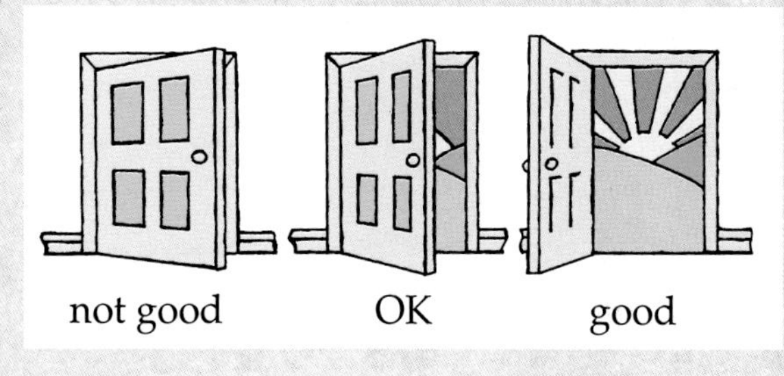

In unit 3 I like ...... I don't like ......

All around the world!

Listen and complete the words of the song. 10

We're brothers and **(1)** ......
Every **(2)** ...... and **(3)** ......
We sing our song of freedom
All around the world!

In Europe and Australia
In **(4)** ...... too
In **(5)** ...... and **(6)** ......
We sing our song for you!

4a DO YOU EAT OCTOPUS?

1

1 Nick and his friends are at the Community Centre.
It is lunch-time.

Nick Is there any salad, Mrs Lee?
Mrs Lee Yes, there is, Nick. There's some salad here.
Nick Thanks. Are there any sandwiches?
Mrs Lee No, there aren't any sandwiches today. Sorry!

2 **Nick** Would you like some fruit, Ana?
Ana Yes, please.
Gary Would you like a Coke?
Ana No, thanks. Just water, please.

3 **Gary** Do you like fish and chips, Ana?
Ana Yes, I do and I like apple pie. But I don't like hamburgers.
Gary Ana, is it true? Do Spanish people eat octopus?
Ana Yes, we do!
Nick Ugh! Octopus? Horrible!

4 **Ana** My boyfriend likes English food.
Nick Your boyfriend? Does he come from Spain?
Ana No, he doesn't. He's Greek. Do you remember Petros?
Nick Oh, yes. Is he your boyfriend?
Ana Yes, he is.
Nick Oh!

Comprehension

1 **Look at the menu and answer the questions. Use**
Yes, there is. **or** ***No, there isn't.***
Yes, there are. **or** ***No, there aren't.***

Is there any soup today?
Yes, there is.

1 Is there any fruit juice today?
2 Is there any vegetable soup today?
3 Is there any apple pie today?
4 Are there any sandwiches today?
5 Are there any apples today?
6 Are there any oranges today?

2 **Answer the questions. Use**
Yes, she/he does. **or** ***No, she/he doesn't.***
Yes, they do. **or** ***No, they don't.***

Does Ana like fish and chips?
Yes, she does.

1 Does Ana like hamburgers?
2 Does Ana like apple pie?
3 Do Nick and Gary like octopus?
4 Does Petros like English food?
5 Do Spanish people eat octopus?
6 Do Ana and Petros come from Greece?

Communication

Likes and dislikes

3 **Make two lists. Use the food and drink in the pictures below.**

✔ *I like*		✘ *I don't like*	
food	*drink*	*food*	*drink*
......	......	......	......

4 **Listen and repeat.** 🎧 2

Ana Do you like hamburgers?
Nick Yes, I do.
Ana Do you like fish?
Nick No, I don't.

Now ask your friend about food and drink. Use the words in exercise 3.

Offering, accepting and refusing

5 **Listen and repeat.** 🎧 3

Sara Would you like a sandwich?
Gary Yes, please.
Sara Would you like a Coke?
Gary No, thanks.

Now ask and answer with a friend.

an apple   a hamburger   a Pepsi
an orange   a cup of coffee   *You choose!*

Pronunciation

6 **Listen and repeat.** 🎧 4

long /ɔː/	short /ɒ/
sports	sorry
your	octopus
water	horrible

Listen, repeat and write. Is each sound long or short?

1 four   2 coffee   3 not   4 August

4b Grammar

Present simple tense (negative and interrogative)

1 Study the table. What are the missing words?

Regular verbs: present simple tense

affirmative	negative		interrogative		
			questions	short answers	
	full forms	*short forms*		*affirmative*	*negative*
I you like	I you ▢ like	I you ▢ like	▢ I you like ...?	Yes, I you ▢.	No, I you ▢.
she he likes it	she he ▢ like it	she he ▢ like it	▢ she he like ...? it	Yes, she he ▢. it	No, she he ▢. it
we you like they	we you ▢ like they	we you ▢ like they	▢ we you like ...? they	Yes, we you ▢. they	No, we you ▢. they

2 Complete the sentences in your notebook. Use *doesn't* or *don't*.

Sue ...... like fish.

Sue doesn't like fish.

1 Sue and Linda ...... live in Spain.
2 Sue's brother ...... work in London.
3 Linda's friends ...... eat octopus.
4 'You ...... study Chinese, Sue!'
5 'We ...... study Portuguese,' says Linda.
6 Mike ...... like Maths.

3 Complete the questions. Use *Does...?* or *Do...?* Then write the answers. Use *doesn't* or *don't*.

...... Linda's friends eat octopus?

Q Do Linda's friends eat octopus?

A No, they don't.

1 ...... Sue like fish?
2 ...... Linda and Sue study Portuguese?
3 ...... Sue study Chinese?
4 ...... Sue's brother work in London?
5 ...... Sue and Linda live in Spain?
6 ...... Mike like Maths?

4 Linda asks you six questions. Write her questions and then give true answers.

...... you eat octopus?

Q Do you eat octopus?

A Yes, I do. or *No, I don't.*

1 ...... you like hamburgers?
2 ...... your English teacher like tea?
3 ...... you and your family live in Spain?
4 ...... your Maths teacher work in Greece?
5 ...... you like football?
6 ...... your mother like jazz?

Countable and uncountable nouns

5 **Study the table.**

countable nouns		**uncountable nouns**
singular	*plural*	*singular only*
tomato	tomato**es**	cheese
orange	orange**s**	tea
sandwich	sandwich**es**	soup

What's the difference? Complete the rules.

1 Countable nouns are singular AND ......

2 Uncountable nouns are ONLY ......

6 **Add these words to the lists. Use** ***pizza, cheese, egg, Coke, hamburger, fruit, chip, water, pea, salt.***

countable nouns		uncountable nouns
singular	*plural*	*singular*
pizza	pizzas	

Learn this!

Countable nouns

There are **some** apples.
There aren't **any** apples.
Are there **any** apples?

Uncountable nouns

There's **some** water.
There isn't **any** water.
Is there **any** water?

7 **What's the difference between** ***some*** **and** ***any*****? Complete the rules.**

1 Use ...... with affirmative sentences.

2 Use ...... with negative sentences.

3 Use ...... with interrogative sentences (questions).

8 **What's in the fridge? Complete the sentences. Use** ***some*** **or** ***any*****.**

There's ...... water.
There's some water.

1 There's ...... milk.

2 There are ...... vegetables.

3 There aren't ...... eggs.

4 There isn't ...... cheese.

5 There aren't ...... sandwiches.

6 There are ...... oranges.

7 There isn't ...... tea.

9 **Write questions and answers about food and drink in the fridge.**

Q Is there any coffee in the fridge?
A No, there isn't.

Q Are there any apples in the fridge?
A Yes, there are.

Study skills

New words

10 **Learn some new words every day.**

Monday	Tuesday
CLASSROOM OBJECTS	FOOD
map	hamburger
ruler	fish
desk	orange

4c Vocabulary

Food and drink

1 An accident at the supermarket! Listen and repeat. 🎧5

1 *Here's the bread.* 2 *Here are the bananas.*

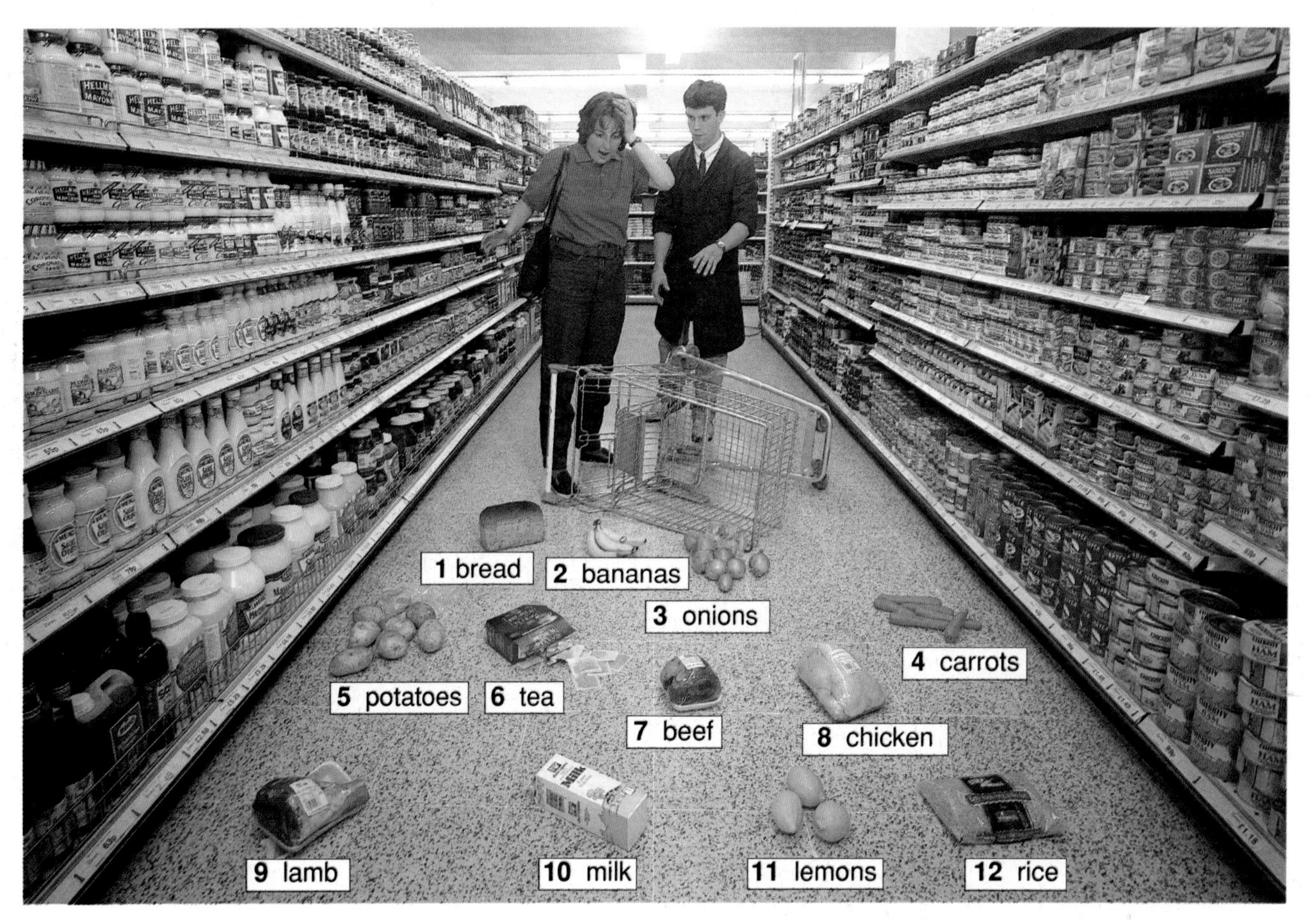

2 Copy and complete the diagram.

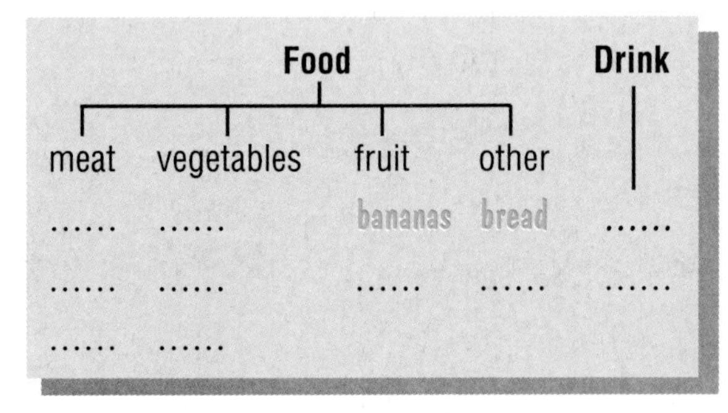

3 Change the pictures into words. Then practise the dialogue with a partner.

Child I'm hungry. I want some

1 

Parent There isn't any. Would you like a

2  ?

Child No. Are there any 3  ?

Parent No. Would you like a 4  ?

Child No, but are there any 5  ?

Parent No, there aren't. But there's an

6 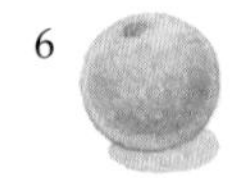 in the fridge.

Child No, thanks. I'm not hungry now.

English across the curriculum

Mathematics

1 **Complete Mike's blackboard in your notebook. Use words from Linda's blackboard.**

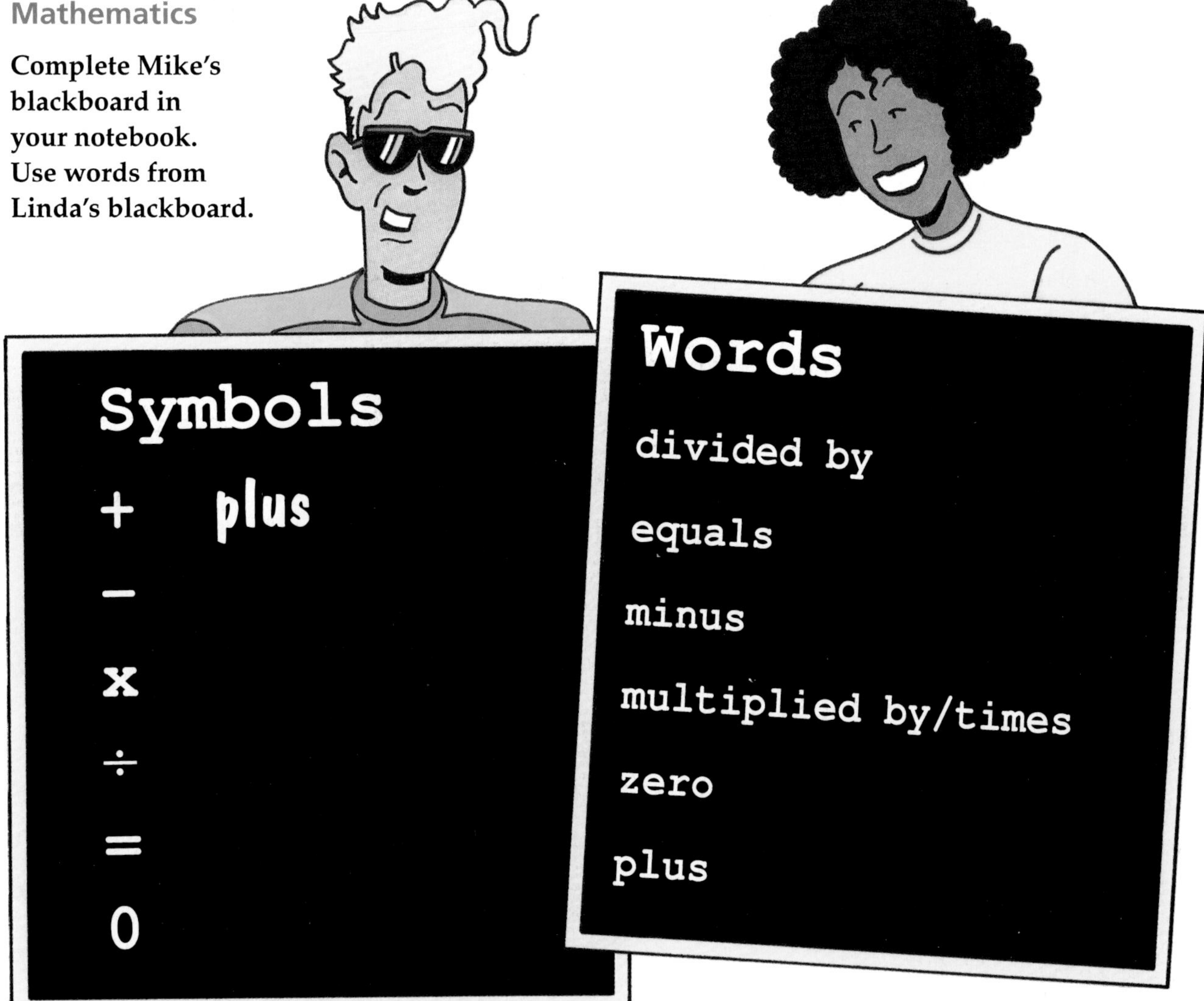

2 **What are the missing numbers? Say the sums. Then write the sums in words.**

4 + 8 = 12

Four plus eight equals twelve.

1 19 – ...... = 9

2 ...... x 3 = 15

3 20 ÷ 5 = ...

4 12 + 4 – 8 x 2 ÷ 4 = ...

3 **What are the missing symbols? Say the sums. Then write the sums in words.**

3 x 8 = 24

Three times eight equals twenty-four.

1 33 ...... 11 = 3

2 12 ...... 15 = 27

3 30 ...... 9 = 21

4 18 ...... 2 ...... 1 ...... 3 ...... 6 = 24

4 **Complete the puzzle with the missing symbols. Then write the answers.**

Twelve plus four equals sixteen.

12	+	4	=	16
	■		■	
3		2		6
	■		■	
4		6		10

4d Skills work

Reading

1 Read the text and the menu.

In British schools, there are lessons in the morning and in the afternoon. Many children eat lunch at school.

In this school, there are two kinds of soup today. The soup costs forty pence. There are three main courses. They cost one pound twenty-five pence. There are two desserts. They are fifty pence. There is a selection of drinks. They are thirty pence.

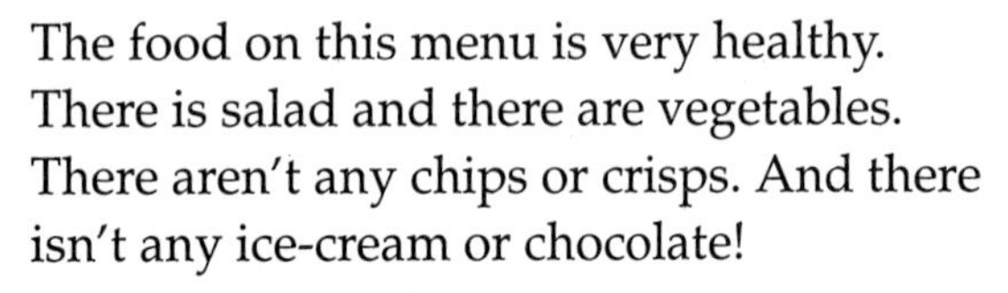

The food on this menu is very healthy. There is salad and there are vegetables. There aren't any chips or crisps. And there isn't any ice-cream or chocolate!

Some children in British schools do not eat pork, and some children do not eat any meat. These children choose a vegetarian meal. Today there is vegetarian pie or salad for these children.

Monday 12 December
Your menu and prices for today

◆◆◆

Soup — *40p*
Vegetable
Tomato

◆◆◆

Main courses — *£1.25*
Meat pie
Vegetarian pie
Salad

◆◆◆

Vegetables — *30p*
Carrots
Peas

◆◆◆

Desserts — *50p*
Fresh fruit
Lemon pie

◆◆◆

Drinks — *30p*
Milk
Diet Pepsi
Water (free)

◆◆◆

Have a good meal!

2 True or false? Write the answers in your notebook.

In British schools, there are lessons in the morning, but not in the afternoon.
False. There are lessons in the morning and in the afternoon.

1 There are three kinds of soup on the menu.
2 The soup costs forty pence.
3 There are two desserts on the menu.
4 The desserts cost forty pence.
5 A drink of milk costs thirty pence.
6 The food on the menu is not healthy.
7 There is ice-cream on the menu.
8 Some children choose a vegetarian meal at school.

Listening

3 Listen to Keith. What does he choose? How much money does he pay? 6

SOUP	Tomato	40p
MAIN COURSE	......	......
VEGETABLES	......	......
DESSERT	......	......
DRINK	......	
TOTAL		......

Speaking

4 Asking about prices. Ask and answer about the prices on the menu.

You How much is ...?
Partner It's ...
or
You How much does ... cost?
Partner It costs ...

Progress Diary 4

Grammar

1 Complete the table in your notebook.

The present simple tense

I like	I don't like	Do I like?
You like	……	……
She likes	……	……

2 Add four nouns to each list.

countable		uncountable
orange	oranges	milk
……	……	……

3 Complete the sentences with *some* or *any*.

There are …… books on the desk.

There aren't …… maps on the wall.

Are there …… cassettes on the table?

Vocabulary

4 Write six words for food and four words for drink.

Food	*Drink*
potatoes	water
……	……

Write the words.

+	−	x	÷	=
plus	……	……	……	……

Communication

5 How do you say these in your language?

Q Do you like hamburgers?

A Yes, I do. **or** No, I don't.

offering Would you like some fruit?

accepting Yes, please.

refusing No, thanks.

Q How much does the soup cost?

A It costs forty pence.

Pronunciation

6 Complete the table. Use *coffee, forty, Paul, cost, water, not.*

long /ɔː/	**short /ɒ/**
forty	……
……	……
……	……

My progress

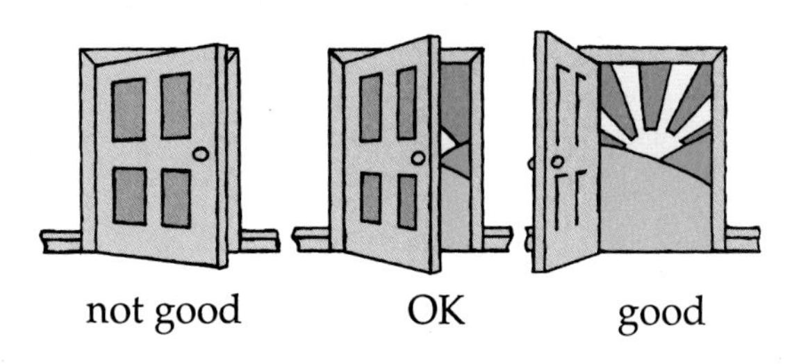

In unit 4 I like …… I don't like ……

One, two, one, two, three!

Listen and repeat. 7

One, two, one, two, three!
Tea, tea, is there any tea?

Four, five, four, five, six!
Chips, chips, are there any chips?

Seven, eight, seven, eight, nine!
Wine, wine, is there any wine?

Boys, girls, women and men!
Nine, ten, start again!

5a NO, YOU CAN'T!

1

(1) It is ten o'clock on Saturday morning, 14 January. Sara and Tina are at Gary's house.

Gary Hi, Nick! Can we come to your house?
Nick Yes, you can. No problem.

(2) Gary and the girls are at Nick's house. It's a quarter past ten.

Nick Mum, can we listen to some music in my room?
Mum No, you can't.
Nick Can we go in the living-room?
Mum No, you can't. You can go in the garage. You can stay there until lunch, at half past twelve.

(3) It's a quarter to one.

Sara Nick! There's a man with a dog!
Nick Oh no! It's Dad. What's the time?

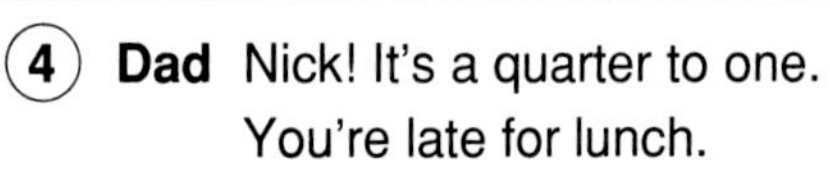

(4) **Dad** Nick! It's a quarter to one. You're late for lunch.
Nick But, Dad. Can we ...?
Dad No, you can't! Not another word. Your mum's angry.
Nick Parents!

Comprehension

1 True or false?

Gary can go to Nick's house. True.

1 Nick can listen to cassettes in his room.
2 Nick can't listen to cassettes in the living-room.
3 Nick can't listen to cassettes in the garage.
4 Nick can stay in the garage until one o'clock.

Communication

Talking about the time

2 Listen and repeat. 2

It's nine o'clock. *It's five past nine.*

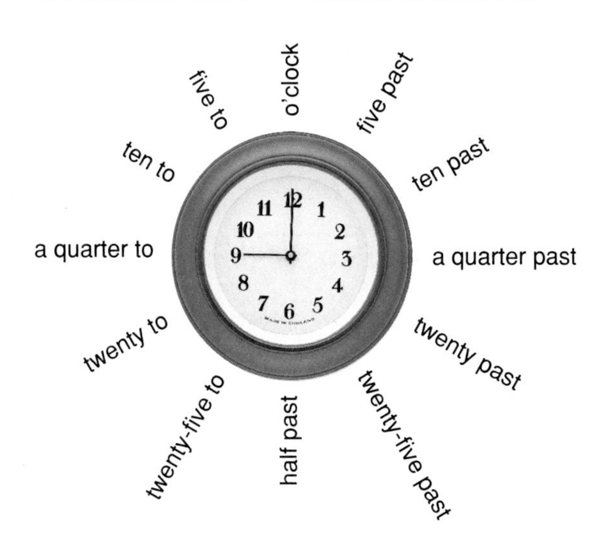

3 Ask and answer about the time.

Nick What's the time?

Sara It's a quarter past nine.

You choose!

4 Listen and repeat. 3

Sara **What time** does your mum eat breakfast?

Nick She eats breakfast at half past seven.

Sara **When** do you go to bed?

Nick I go to bed at half past ten.

Now ask and answer about you and your family.

get up   eat lunch   do your homework
watch TV   leave school   ***You choose!***

Talking about permission

5 Write true sentences.

At home I can ...... but I can't ......

watch TV until eleven o'clock
eat ice-cream for breakfast
play loud music in my room
You choose!

At school we can ...... but we can't ......

play football
use a dictionary in English lessons
listen to pop music
You choose!

Pronunciation

6 Listen and repeat. 4

long /ɜː/	short /e/
girls	ten
word	yes

Listen, repeat and write. Is each sound long or short?

1 third   **2** men   **3** Wednesday
4 learn

5b Grammar

Revision of present simple tense

1 **Use the diagram to help you write questions and answers in your notebook.**

Q Do your parents speak English?

A No, they don't.

Q Does your brother play football?

A Yes, he does.

2 **True or false?**

	hamburgers	salad	fish	ice-cream
Linda	✘	✔	✔	✔
Sue	✔	✔	✘	✘
Mike	✔	✔	✘	✔

Linda likes fish.

True.

1 Sue likes salad.
2 Mike likes fish.
3 Linda and Mike like salad.
4 Sue doesn't like ice-cream.
5 Linda doesn't like ice-cream.
6 Sue and Mike don't like hamburgers.

3 **Write questions and then give the answers.**

Sue and Mike / eat / fish?

Q Do Sue and Mike eat fish?

A No, they don't.

1 Sue / eat / ice-cream?
2 Linda and Mike / eat / ice-cream?
3 Sue / eat / hamburgers?
4 Linda / eat / hamburgers?
5 Mike / eat / hamburgers and salad?
6 Linda and Mike / eat / salad and ice-cream?

The verb *can*

4 **Study the forms of *can*.**

affirmative		I **can** listen to music in my bedroom.
negative	*full form* *short form*	She **cannot** listen to music in the living-room. He **can't** listen to music in the kitchen.
interrogative		**Q** **Can** we listen to music in the dining-room? **A** Yes, you **can**. or No, you **can't**.

5 **Listen and repeat.** 🎧 5

Nick Can I go to a party on Saturday?

Mum Yes, you can.

Nick Can I stay at the party until midnight?

Dad No, you can't.

Now ask and answer. Your partner is Mum or Dad.

You Can I ...?

Partner Yes, you can. **or** No, you can't.

stay in bed until eleven o'clock

go to London with my friends

watch the football match on TV

watch TV until midnight

You choose!

Study skills

Memorizing

6 **Copy and complete the lists. Then listen, repeat and memorize.** 🎧 6

1st first

2nd second

3rd third

4th fourth

5th ......

↓

10th tenth

11th eleventh

12th twelfth

13th thirteenth

...... fourteenth

....

↓

20th twentieth

21st twenty-first

22nd twenty-second

23rd twenty-third

...... twenty-fourth

....

↓

30th thirtieth

31st thirty-first

7 **Ask and answer.**

You What's the date today?

Partner It's Monday, June the thirteenth.

5c Vocabulary

Houses and homes

1 **Study the picture of Sir Edward's house in the country. Listen and repeat the words.** 🎧7

2 **Ask and answer.**

You Where's Sir Edward?

Partner He's in the …

the thief? the policeman?

the piano? the dog?

You choose!

3 **Listen. Where's the thief?** 🎧8

He's in the bedroom!

1 …… **2** …… **3** …… **4** ……

Learn this!

in the bedroom — **on** the stairs
in the garden — **on** the roof
in the shower

English across the curriculum

Cross-cultural studies: houses and homes around the world

1 Traditional homes. Match the words with the pictures.

igloo
tepee
tent

Modern homes. Match the words with the photos.

farm
flats
house

2 Read about three young people, then answer the questions.

1 Who lives in a large city?
2 Who lives in the country?
3 Who lives by the sea?

Kirk is American. He lives on a farm. It is near a small town.

Mary is Nigerian. She lives in a large house. It is near the Atlantic Ocean.

Peter is Hungarian. He lives in a small flat. It is in Budapest.

3 Listen. Copy and complete the table. 9

Name		Kirk	Mary	Peter
Nationality		American		
Type of home		farm		
Inside	Number of rooms	seven		
	Number of bedrooms	three		
Outside	Is there a garden?	Yes		
	Is there a garage?	Yes		
Place	Country	Yes		
	Sea	No		
	City	No		

5d Skills work

Reading

1 Answer these questions and then read about this home.

1 Do you live in a house or a flat?

2 Is your house

   a) in a city, town or village?

   b) in the country?

   c) by the sea?

Hello. My name is Karen. This is my grandparents' flat. They live in Brighton. Brighton is a large town in the south of England. It is on the south coast of England.

My grandparents' flat is on the second floor. The flat is by the sea. The flat is small. There is a kitchen and a living-room. There are two bedrooms, and a small bathroom with a toilet. There isn't a garden or a garage but there is a balcony. My brother and I like our grandparents' flat. We go there for our holidays. It's great!

2 Complete the notes about the home in Brighton.

1 Type of home   flat

2 Place   ......

3 Inside   ......

4 Outside   ......

Group work

3 In groups make notes about your dream home.

1 Type ......

2 Place ......

3 Inside ......

4 Outside ......

Speaking

4 Use your notes to make a short speech about your dream home.

Our dream home is ......

Writing

5 Change your notes and your speech into a short composition 'My dream home'. Include a plan or a photo with your composition!

Progress Diary 5

Grammar

1 Change the affirmative sentences to negative.

He likes cheese.

They live in the country.

She can play loud music.

Change the affirmative sentences to interrogative.

He eats breakfast at eight o'clock.

They live in a large town.

She can watch TV until midnight.

2 Complete the phrases. Use *in, at, on.*

...... home	...... the stairs
...... bed	...... the kitchen
...... the country	...... the farm

Vocabulary

3 Answer these questions about rooms.

Where's the bed?	In the ......
Where's the bath?	In the ......
Where's the car?	In the ......
Where's the cooker?	In the ......

Communication

4 Ask and answer about time.

Q What's the time?

A It's	6.00	10.10	in the morning.
	2.30	3.20	in the afternoon.
	7.40	8.25	in the evening.

5 Talking about permission
Write two things you can do at home.

I can ......

Write two things you can't do at school.

I can't ......

Pronunciation

6 Complete the table. Use *bed, first, tent, Thursday, girl, yes.*

long /ɜː/	short /e/
first	......
......	......
......	......

My progress

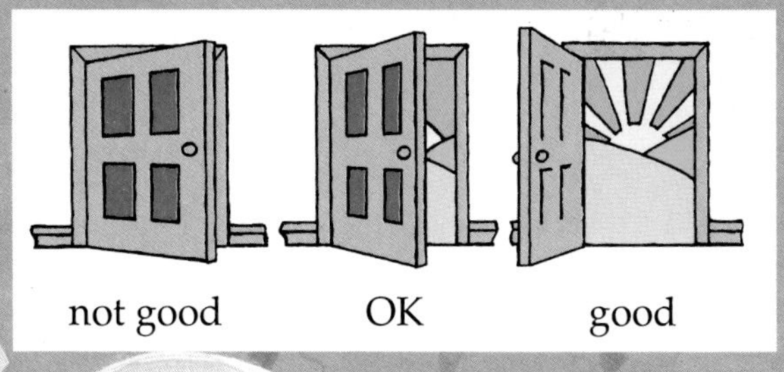

In unit 5 I like ...... I don't like ......

Gordon the Ghost!

Listen and complete the words of the song. 10

My name is Gordon
I'm upstairs and I'm down
I'm (1) ...... and I'm (2) ......
Tonight I'm in your town!

Now I'm in your (3) ......
Now I'm in your (4) ......
Now I'm in your (5) ......
Now I'm on the stair!

Now I'm in your (6) ......
Now I'm in your (7) ......
Now I'm in your (8) ......
Where are you?

6a SPORTS CLOTHES

1

(1) Nick has got a grey tracksuit. He has also got a pair of white shorts, a pair of blue trainers and a black baseball cap. And he's got two T-shirts – a green one and a blue one. But now Nick is in the school basketball team and the team's colour is red!

(2) **Nick** Have you got any red T-shirts?
Assistant Sure. There's one up here.
Nick Have you got any red shorts?
Assistant No, I'm sorry, we haven't. But we've got some blue ones.
Nick No, thanks. I want red ones.

(3) **Assistant** Be careful! Don't touch those tennis rackets!
Nick Sorry!

(4) **Nick** Oh, hello, Sara!
Sara Hello, Nick! I'm in the school hockey team, but I haven't got any red sports clothes.
Nick I've got the same problem.

Comprehension

1 Answer the questions.

What colour is Nick's baseball cap?

Black.

1 What colour is Nick's tracksuit?
2 What colour are Nick's shorts?
3 What colour are Nick's trainers?
4 What colour are Nick's T-shirts?

2 Answer the questions with full answers.

Has Nick got a red T-shirt?

No, he hasn't. He's got a green one and a blue one.

1 Has Nick got a green baseball cap?
2 Has Nick got a pair of white shorts?
3 Has Nick got a pair of blue trainers?
4 Has Nick got a green tracksuit?

Communication

Instructions

3 Match the instructions with the pictures.

Be careful! This water is hot.

Don't be late!

Insert 50p here.

Don't leave money or valuables.

1

2

3

4

Talking about possession

4 Listen and repeat. 2

Sara Have you got a tracksuit?
Nick Yes, I have.
Sara What colour is it?
Nick It's grey.

Nick Have you got a pair of trainers?
Sara Yes, I have.
Nick What colour are they?
Sara They're white.

5 Make a list of your clothes and their colours. Then ask and answer.

You Have you got ...?
Partner Yes, I have. **or** No, I haven't.
You What colour is it / are they?
Partner It's/They're ...

Pronunciation

6 Listen and repeat. 3

short /ʌ/	short /æ/
London	black
up	rackets
touch	cap

Listen, repeat and write. Is each sound short /ʌ/ or short /æ/?

1 mum 2 man
3 colour 4 angry

6b Grammar

The verb *have got*

1 Study the forms of the verb *have got*.

		I, you, we, they	she, he, it
affirmative	*full form* *short form*	I **have got** a blue T-shirt. **I've got** a blue T-shirt.	She **has got** a green scarf. She'**s got** a green scarf.
negative	*full form* *short form*	I **have not got** a red T-shirt. I **haven't got** a red T-shirt.	She **has not got** a grey scarf. She **hasn't got** a grey scarf.
interrogative		**Q Have** you **got** a white T-shirt? **A** Yes, I **have**. or No, I **haven't**.	**Q Has** she **got** a black scarf? **A** Yes, she **has**. or No, she **hasn't**.

2 Complete the sentences in your notebook. Use the correct affirmative form of the verb *have got*. Use full forms.

Darren ...... a black baseball cap.

Darren has got a black baseball cap.

1 Sue ...... a red baseball cap.

3 Darren and Sue ...... blue jackets.

2 Darren ...... a white scarf.

4 Sue and Darren ...... blue T-shirts.

5 Sue ...... a blue-and-white scarf.

3 Complete the sentences with the correct negative form of the verb *have got*. Use short forms.

Sue ...... a blue baseball cap.

Sue hasn't got a blue baseball cap.

1 Sue and Darren ...... green jackets.

2 Darren ...... a white baseball cap.

3 Sue ...... a grey scarf.

4 Darren and Sue ...... red jeans.

5 Darren ...... a green scarf.

4 Write questions with the verb *have got*. Then answer the questions with short answers.

Sue / blue baseball cap?

Q Has Sue got a blue baseball cap?

A No, she hasn't.

1 Darren / black baseball cap?

2 Sue and Darren / green jackets?

3 Darren and Sue / blue T-shirts?

4 Sue / red baseball cap?

5 Darren / black scarf?

Imperatives

5 Learn how to make imperatives. Then match Darren's instructions with the pictures.

	affirmative	*negative*
be	Be quiet!	Don't be stupid!
all other verbs	Follow me!	Don't forget the tickets!

1

2

3

4

The pronoun *one/ones*

6 Listen and repeat. 🎧 4

Sue I don't like this white baseball cap. Have you got a red one?

Darren These pens are black. Are there any blue ones?

7 Complete the sentences. Use *one* or *ones*.

I don't like this green T-shirt. Have you got a blue one (blue)?

1. These tennis rackets are expensive. Are there ...... (cheap)?
2. This map is small. I'd like ...... (big).
3. I'd like a hamburger. But I don't want ...... (cold)!
4. These oranges are big. Have you got ...... (small)?
5. These red pens are OK. But I'd like ...... (green).

Study skills

Using vocabulary topics

8 Add three words to each vocabulary list. Compare your words with your partner.

9 Choose your favourite topic and write five words about it. Share your words with the class.

pop music food travel sport

You choose!

6c Vocabulary

Clothes

1 **Look at Sue Brown's family album. Listen and repeat the words for clothes.** 🎧 5

2 **Listen and repeat the names of the colours.** 🎧 6

Me in the mountains!

Paul on holiday

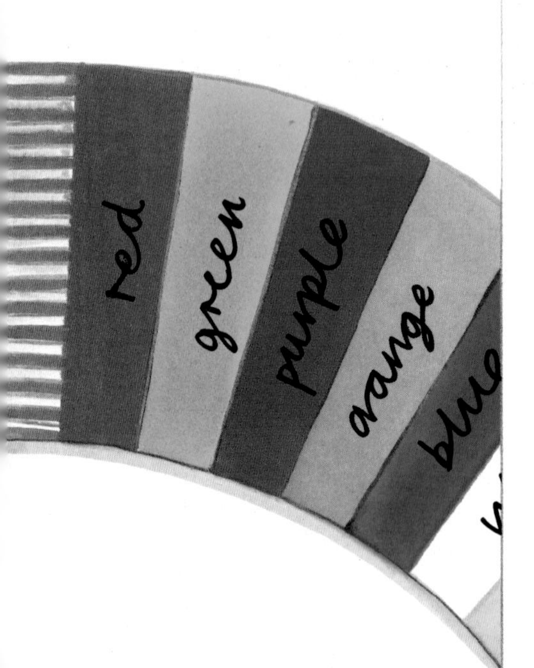

Mum at work!

Dad at Aunt Ann's Wedding

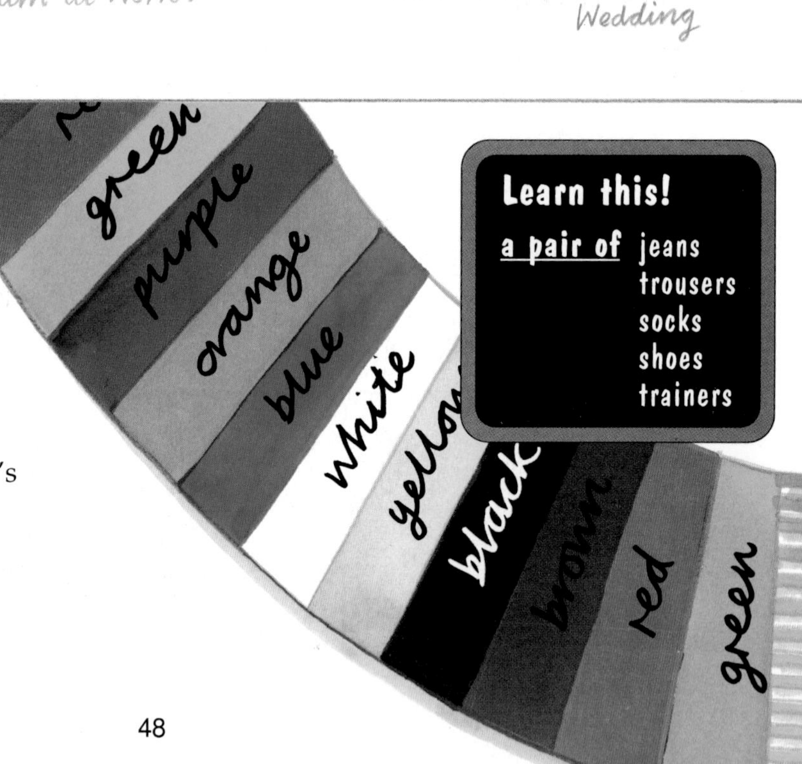

Learn this!

a pair of jeans
trousers
socks
shoes
trainers

3 **Ask and answer about the Browns' clothes.**

You What colour is Sue's sweater?

Partner It's green.

You What colour are Mr Brown's trousers?

Partner They're black.

4 **Describe your clothes to a friend.**

I've got ......

English across the curriculum

Natural science: animals in danger!

1

Redwood School is in a village near the ancient city of York. The school curriculum includes lessons about natural science. The lessons are on Friday mornings. The students have got some interesting books and videos about the environment.

The school has got a video about animals and wildlife. It is called *Animals in danger*. The video teaches the students about rare animals, for example, pandas, elephants, and tigers. A student in year eight has also got a video. Her video is a television programme about the world's oceans. It shows that dolphins and whales and other animals in the sea are in danger.

The students do projects in their natural science lessons. They make posters about the environment and they write articles for the school magazine. The articles about animals and the environment are very popular.

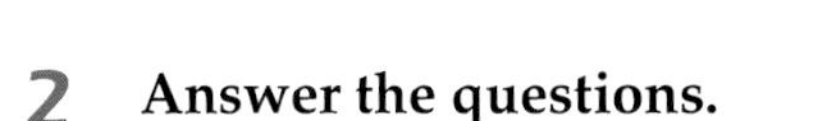

2 Answer the questions.

Where is Redwood school?

It is in a village near the ancient city of York.

1. When are the natural science lessons?
2. What is the name of the video about animals and wildlife?
3. Who has got a video about the world's oceans?
4. What animals are in danger?
5. What do the students write in their natural science lessons?

3 Match each slogan with its correct poster. Choose from

Save the elephant! *Protect the panda!*
Don't forget the rainforests!
Don't destroy the oceans!

1

2

3 4

6d Skills work

Listening

1 **Listen to the conversations. What pets has each person got? Copy and complete the table in your notebook.** 🎧 7

Speaking

2 **Talk about Anne, Dave and Frances, and their pets.**

Anne has got ......

Reading

3 **Read the text and answer the questions below.**

	Anne	Dave	Frances
dog			
cat			
horse	1		
rabbit			
tortoise	1		
hamster			
canary			

The British love animals. Many families have got one or two pets. Their pets are part of the family. Popular pets are dogs, cats, and birds.

Some people have got very unusual pets. Emma is a teenager. She lives in London. She hasn't got a dog or a cat. She has got a white rat. It is called Winston. 'My friends don't like Winston,' says Emma. 'But he's beautiful. He isn't dangerous. He's very friendly.'

Harry lives in the north of England. He has got a lot of pets. He's got two dogs, three cats, and some canaries. But his favourite pet is a peacock. He's called Henry. 'I love Henry and he loves me,' says Harry. 'I haven't got a wife or children, so I haven't got a real family. My pets are my family. We are very happy.'

Who's got a lot of pets? *Harry.*

1 Who's got a pet called Henry?
2 Who's got a pet rat?
3 Who hasn't got a pet dog?
4 Who hasn't got a real family?

Writing

4 **What pets have you or your friends got? What are they called? Write about them.**

Progress Diary 6

Grammar

1 Complete the sentences with the correct form of *have got*.

affirmative	Anne …… two pets.
negative	Harry …… a real family.
interrogative	…… Frances …… a horse?

2 Write examples of the imperative.

	the verb *to be*	other verbs
affirmative	……	……
negative	……	……

3 Complete the sentences with *one* or *ones*.

I don't want the grey shirt. I want a blue ……

She doesn't like the green shorts. She likes red ……

Vocabulary

4 Name four animals.

panda, ……………………………………

Name five colours.

red, ……………………………………

Name six items of clothing.

trainers, ……………………………………

Communication

5 Write questions and answers about possession. Use *have got*.

you / a video?	Q ……	A ……
your friend / a camera?	Q ……	A ……

Pronunciation

6 Complete the table. Use *colour, panda, rabbit, some, mum, black*.

short /ʌ/	short /æ/
mum	
……	……
……	……

My progress

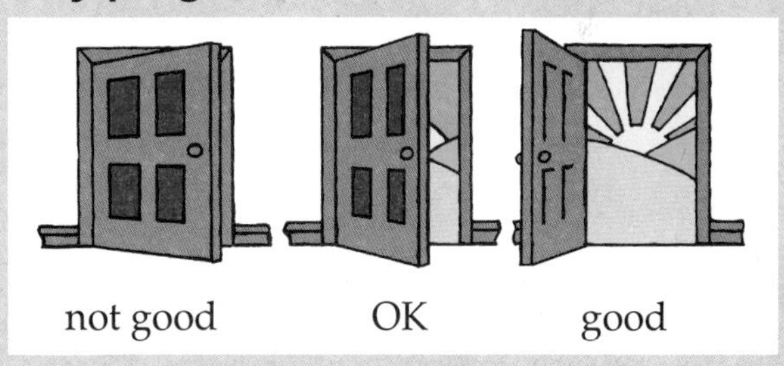

not good OK good

In unit 6	I like ……	I don't like ……

Fashion Queen!

Listen to the song. Put the three verses into their correct order. 8

A She's got long red boots
She's got blue blue jeans
She's got a long long sweater
Do you know what I mean?

B She's a real hot scene
She's a teenage dream
Go, girl, go!
You're a fashion queen.

C She walks like a cat
She sings like a bird
She wears great clothes
She's a real cool girl.

7a AT THE SPORTS CENTRE

1

① Nick and his friends go to the Sports and Leisure Centre twice a week, every Tuesday and Thursday. Ana also goes to the Centre. She goes there once a week, on Thursdays.

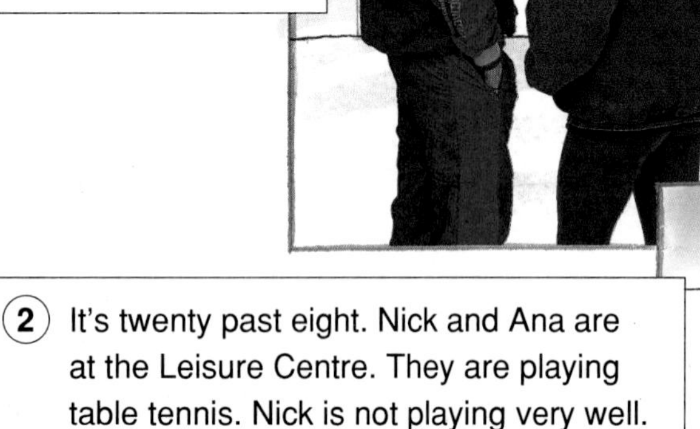

② It's twenty past eight. Nick and Ana are at the Leisure Centre. They are playing table tennis. Nick is not playing very well. He is losing the game!

Nick You're playing very well this evening, Ana.

❸ Sara and her friends are playing football. Sara is playing for the red team. Lucy is playing for the blue team.

Sara Goal! Hooray! We're winning.
Lucy Sara! Don't kick me.
Referee What's the problem, Lucy?
Lucy It's Sara. She's kicking me!
Sara No, I'm not! You're pushing me!
Referee Stop the game!

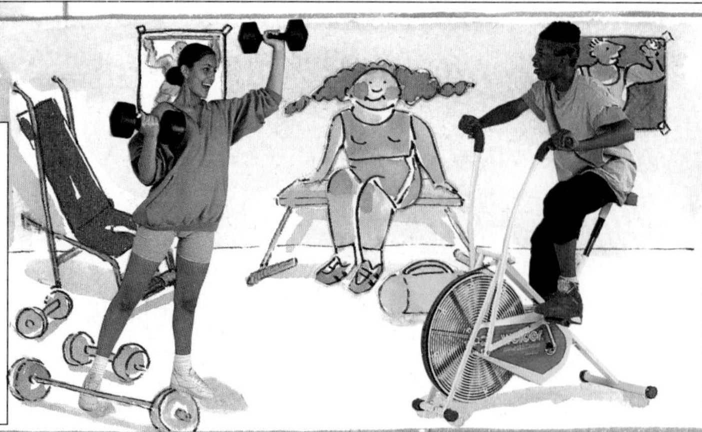

④ Gary and Tina are not playing table tennis or football. They are weight-training.

Gary You can't lift those!
Tina Yes, I can!
Gary But girls can't lift weights!
Tina Yes, we can. Look!
Gary Wow!

Comprehension

1 Complete the conversations in your notebook.

Ana When do you and your friends go to the Sports Centre, Nick?

Nick We go ...... a week, every ...... and ......

Sara How often do you go, Ana?

Ana I go ...... a week, on ......

2 It's twenty past eight. True or false?

Nick is playing table tennis.
True.

1 Ana is playing table tennis.
2 Nick is winning.
3 Gary is playing football.
4 Tina is weight-training.
5 Sara and the red team are winning.
6 Sara is kicking Lucy.

Communication

Talking about present actions

3 Listen and repeat. 2

He is swimming.

They are playing football.

Now say what these people are doing.

Talking about abilities

4 Listen and repeat. 3

Nick Can you play table tennis?

Ana Yes, I can!

Nick Can you stand on your head?

Ana No, I can't!

Now ask and answer.

play tennis | do a cartwheel | do a handstand

whistle

do this

You choose!

Pronunciation

5 Listen and repeat. 4

The weak vowel /ə/	
the	problem
and	Sara
a	Tina

Centre
Leisure Centre
the Leisure Centre
at the Leisure Centre
are at the Leisure Centre
Tina and Sara are at the Leisure Centre

Listen, repeat and write. Circle the weak vowel /ə/.

1 Saturday 2 December
3 table 4 Open Doors!

7b Grammar

The present continuous tense (affirmative and negative)

1 Complete the table.

affirmative		**negative**	
full forms	*short forms*	*full forms*	*short forms*
I am playing	I'm playing	I am not playing	I'm not playing
you are listening	you're listening	you are not listening	you aren't listening
she is watching	she's	she is not watching	she isn't ......
he is working	......	he is not working	......
it is raining	......	it is not raining	......
we are learning	......	we are not learning	......
you are studying	......	you are not studying	......
they are waiting	......	they are not waiting	......

2 Work out the spelling rules for the *-ing* form of verbs.

Rule 1		**Rule 2**		**Rule 3**	
most verbs		*verbs ending with 'e'*		*some verbs ending with 1 vowel + 1 consonant*	
play	playing	dance	dancing	swim	swimming
listen	listening	live	living	run	running
learn	learning	come	coming	sit	sitting

3 Imagine you are Linda. You are talking to Mike on the phone. Tell Mike what you are doing.

Mike Hi, Linda! What are you doing?

Linda Oh, it's really boring. Mum's ...... TV. (watch)

Mum's watching TV.

1 Dad ...... in his chair. (sit)
2 My sister ...... in her bedroom. (dance)
3 The dog ...... in his basket. (sleep)
4 I ...... my homework. (do)
5 My brothers? They ...... some new cassettes. (listen to)

The present simple tense and the present continuous tense

4 **Compare the meanings.**

present simple = regular habits, routines
They watch TV every day. She plays basketball twice a week. I don't drink Coke.

present continuous = present actions
They're watching TV now. Look! She's playing basketball now. And I'm not drinking Coke now.

5 **Write true sentences about your regular habits. Use the present simple tense.**

1 I ......

2 My friend ......

3 My cousins ......

6 **Write true sentences about your present actions. Use the present continuous tense.**

1 I ......

2 My friend ......

3 My cousins ......

7 **Present simple or present continuous? Write the sentences, using the correct form of the verbs.**

1 Look! Sara ...... football with her friends now. (play)

2 Tina and Gary ...... to the Leisure Centre twice a week. (go)

3 Nick's dad ...... at five a.m. every day. (get up)

4 Sara's mum ...... her favourite TV programme at the moment. (watch)

5 I can't come now. We ...... our dinner. (eat)

6 Yes, we ...... a lot of English at the moment. (learn)

Study skills

Learning abbreviations

8 **Listen and repeat.** 5

You What do the letters *a.m.* mean in English?

Partner The letters *a.m.*? They mean 'in the morning'.

Now ask and answer.

p.m. UK USA Mon

Fri Feb Dec

7c Vocabulary

Parts of the body

1 Listen and repeat. Then learn the words. 🎧6

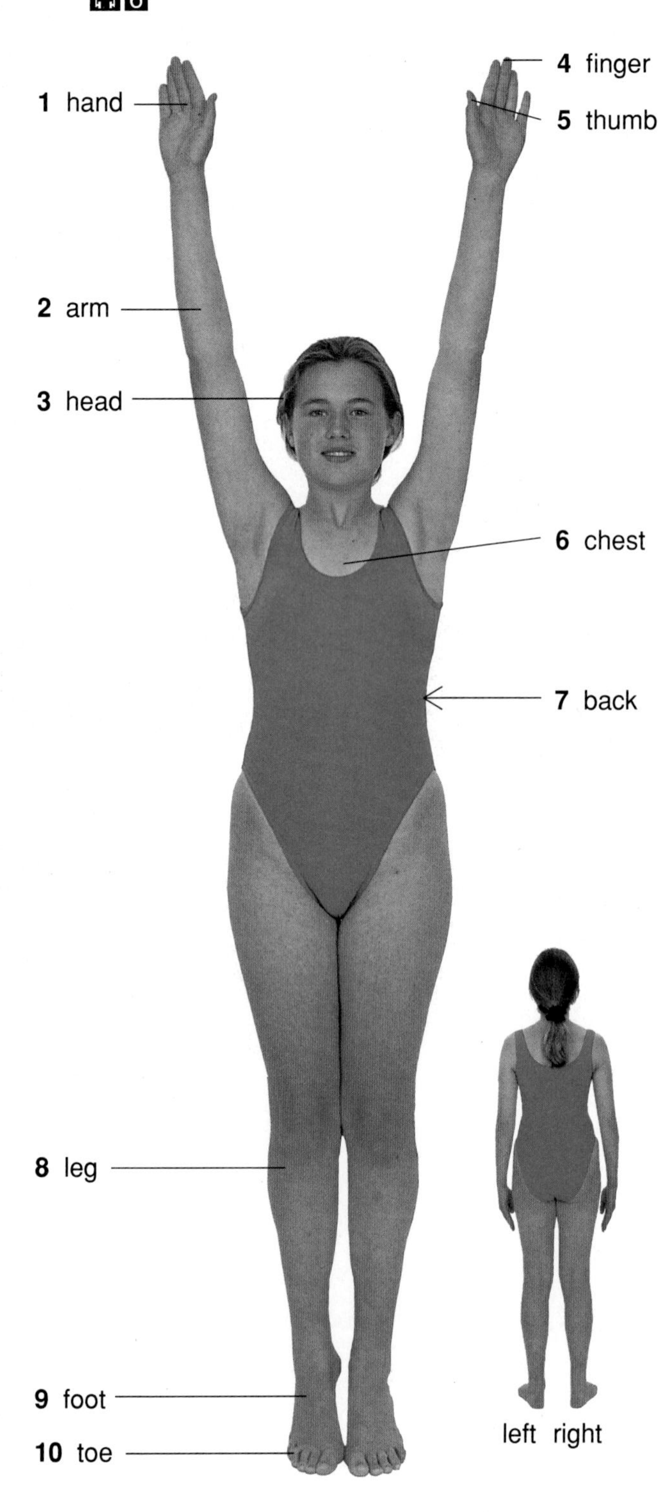

2 Close your book and test your partner.

You What's the English word for this?

Partner 'Head'.

3 Listen to the dictation. Match the words and the numbers. 🎧7

ear eyes face hair lips mouth nose teeth

1 2 3 4 5 6 7 8

4 Test your partner again.

Touch your left eye! Touch your right leg!

You choose!

5 Listen to the patients and their doctor. Who is phoning? 🎧8

1st patient Kevin 3rd patient ......

2nd patient ...... 4th patient ......

Learn this!

What colour **are** your eyes?

What colour **is** your hair?

English across the curriculum

Physical education: sports and games

1 **Can you name the sports? Match the names with the symbols. Then listen and repeat.** 9

athletics baseball basketball cricket gymnastics
hockey ice-skating rugby sailing volleyball

2 **Read about sports and games at a school in London.**

In the UK, school sports are usually called 'Games'. All schoolchildren attend sports lessons. In many schools, students have 'Games' and other outdoor activities on Wednesday afternoons.

Westminster Comprehensive School is in London. In the first and second years, the outdoor sports are football and hockey in the winter and tennis and cricket in the summer. In the third and fourth years, they concentrate on athletics.

In the fifth year, the students choose their favourite outdoor sport. The boys usually choose football and cricket. The girls usually prefer hockey and tennis.

The students also do a lot of indoor sports and activities. Every Monday, they play basketball. The volleyball club meets on Tuesdays and there is a chess club every Wednesday evening. On Thursday evenings, a lot of the children play table tennis. But Friday evenings are the favourite! On Fridays, they go to the school's very popular Disco Dancing club. There is no school on Saturday. But some students go to the local swimming-pool then.

3 **Copy and complete the notes.**

Sports and activities at Westminster Comprehensive School	
Outdoor	
1st/2nd year (winter)	football, hockey
1st/2nd year (summer)	......
3rd/4th year	......
5th year, boys	......
5th year, girls	......
Indoor	
Monday	basketball
Tuesday	......
Wednesday	......
Thursday	......
Friday	......
Saturday	......

7d Skills work

Listening

1 Listen to Clare's daily routine. Complete the times in your notebook. 10

Well, I get up early. I always get up at (**1**) 6.15 and I have a small breakfast at (**2**) ....

Then, at (**3**) ......, my dad takes me to the swimming pool. I practise every day. I usually leave the pool at (**4**) .... Then I go to school. Our lessons start at (**5**) ...... and I don't go home for lunch. I have my lunch at school.

We finish school at (**6**) ...... and I go to the swimming pool again. I swim from (**7**) ...... to (**8**) .... I usually have supper at (**9**) ...... , then I do my homework or watch TV. I sometimes write letters to my penfriends in Spain and Greece, but I always go to bed at (**10**) .... My friends go to bed at eleven o'clock or midnight! But I want to be a champion swimmer, so I go to bed early.

Reading

2 Choose the correct answers.

1 **How often** does Clare go to the swimming-pool?

a) once a day.

b) twice a day.

c) three times a day.

2 **How long** does Clare practise every day?

a) one hour.

b) two hours.

c) three hours.

3 **How long** does Clare stay at school every day?

a) six hours and forty-five minutes.

b) seven hours.

c) seven hours and fifteen minutes.

Speaking

3 You are an interviewer. Your partner is Clare. Ask and answer five questions about Clare's routine.

4 Now ask your partner about her/his daily routine.

You What time do you ......

Partner I ...... at ......

get up?

have breakfast?

go to school?

have lunch?

have your evening meal?

do your homework?

go to bed?

You choose!

Writing

5 Write a short composition about your daily routine, or your friend's daily routine.

Progress Diary 7

Grammar

1 Write sentences in the present continuous tense.

affirmative	she/play/tennis
full form	......
short form	......
negative	we/listen to/music
full form	......
short form	......

2 Present simple or present continuous?

I ...... lunch at one o'clock. (eat)

I ...... lunch now. (eat)

Nick and Ana ...... table tennis on Thursdays. (play)

Nick and Ana ...... table tennis at the moment. (play)

Vocabulary

3 Name three parts of the body.

arm, ...

Name three parts of the face.

eye, ...

Name your three favourite sports.

football, ...

Communication

4 Write two sentences about your daily routine. Include times.

I get up at seven o'clock every day.

Write two sentences about your present actions.

I'm not playing tennis at the moment.

5 Ability or permission?

I can stand on my head.

You can't watch TV until midnight.

Nick, you can buy a new T-shirt.

Ana can't play basketball.

Pronunciation

6 Underline the weak vowel /ə/ sounds in this sentence.

Sara and Tina are at the Leisure Centre.

My progress

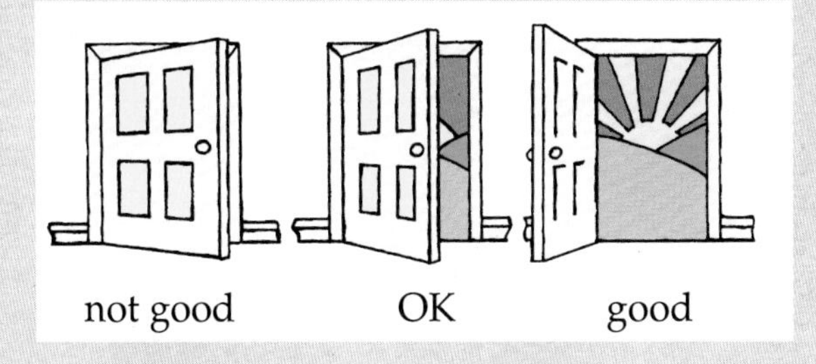

not good OK good

In unit 7 I like ...... I don't like ......

Doing the Hokey Cokey!

Listen. Write the lines of the verse in the correct order. 11

Verse

1 Put your right arm in!
2 ......
3 ...... Shake it all about!
4 ...... In! Out! In! Out!
5 ...... And turn around!
6 ...... Put your right arm in!
7 ...... That's what it's all about!
Put your right arm out!
Do the Hokey Cokey!

Chorus

Oooooh the Hokey Cokey!
Ooooooh the Hokey Cokey!
Oooooooooh the Hokey Cokey!
That's what it's all about!
Oi!

8a WHAT ARE YOU DOING?

1 ① Nick always has his dinner at half past six. After dinner, he often goes upstairs to his room. He usually does his homework there. But sometimes he watches TV in his room. It is a quarter past eight, on Tuesday evening. Nick is in his room. He is watching a TV programme about holidays.

② It is half past eight. Tracy is downstairs. She is feeding Fred. She always feeds Fred at this time. Nick is making a phone call.

Tracy Which girlfriend are you calling? Ana or Sara?

Nick Go away, Tracy! This is a private conversation.

③ Sara is at home. She is doing her homework. A boy from Sara's class often studies with Sara. His name is Ramesh. Ramesh and Sara are studying together this evening. They are finishing a project about the environment.

④ **Sara** Hello!

Nick Hi! It's me, Nick. What are you doing?

Sara I'm writing my project.

Nick Is Ramesh helping you?

Sara Ramesh? No, he isn't.

Nick Yes, he is, Sara. Tell the truth!

Sara Oh, Nick. We're doing a project together. That's all!

Nick I never study with you, Sara. You never invite me to your house!

Comprehension

1 Complete the sentences in your notebook. Use *always, never, often, sometimes, usually*.

1 Nick ...... has his dinner at half past six.
2 Nick ...... goes upstairs after dinner.
3 Nick ...... does his homework in his room.
4 Nick ...... watches TV in his room.
5 Nick ...... studies with Sara.
6 Sara ...... invites Nick to her house.

2 Answer the questions. Write short answers.

When does Nick have his dinner?
At half past six.

1 **Where** does Nick often go after dinner?
2 **How often** does Nick watch TV in his room?
3 **What time** does Tracy feed Fred?
4 **Who** often studies with Sara?
5 **How often** does Sara invite Nick to her house?

Communication

Asking and answering about present actions

3 Listen and repeat the phone conversations. 2

Sara Hi, Gary! What are you doing?
Gary I'm reading a magazine.

Sara Hello, Tina! Are you watching TV?
Tina Yes, I am.

Sara Hi, Nick! Are you listening to the radio?
Nick No, I'm not. I'm washing up.

4 Choose three actions. Don't show your partner. Then ask and answer.

You choose!

Talking about frequency

5 Ask and answer.

You How often do you ...?
Partner Always/Often/Sometimes/Hardly ever/Never

You choose!

Pronunciation

6 Listen and repeat. 3

short /ʌ/	the weak vowel /ə/
supper	Jason
upstairs	often
study	tomorrow

Listen, repeat and write. Is each sound short /ʌ/ or weak vowel /ə/?

1 butter 2 quarter 3 surprise
4 love 5 Sunday 6 Ana

8b Grammar

The present continuous tense (interrogative)

1 Complete the table.

interrogative	short answers	
	affirmative	*negative*
Am I reading?	Yes, I am.	No, I'm not.
Are you listening?	Yes, you are.	No, you aren't.
Is she swimming?	Yes, she is.	No, she isn't.
Is he talking?	Yes, he	......
Is it raining?	......	......
Are we playing?	......	......
Are you working?	......	......
Are they studying?	......	......

2 Write questions and answers about Mike's family.

Joe / play football?

Q Is Joe playing football?

A No, he isn't. He's watching TV.

1 Carol / do her homework?
2 Mr Smith / eat / his dinner?
3 Rex and Queenie / eat their dinner?
4 Mike / do / his science project?
5 Mike's parents / have dinner together?

Question words

3 Translate the question words into your language. Then answer the questions.

1 **Where** do you live?
2 **When** do you get up?
3 **What** time do you go to bed?
4 **What** is your favourite subject?
5 **Who** is your favourite singer?
6 **How** old are you?
7 **How often** do you brush your teeth?
8 **How long** do you stay in the shower?

Adverbs of frequency

4 Translate.

English		Your language
always	✔✔✔✔✔✔✔✔✔✔	......
usually	✔✔✔✔✔✔✔✔✔☐	......
often	✔✔✔✔✔✔✔☐☐☐	......
sometimes	✔✔✔✔✔☐☐☐☐☐	......
hardly ever	✔✔☐☐☐☐☐☐☐☐	......
never	☐☐☐☐☐☐☐☐☐☐	......

5 Write six true sentences about six people in your class. Use adverbs of frequency.

The present simple tense and the present continuous tense

6 Compare the meanings.

Present simple

1 *to express routines, habits*

I get up at 7.00 a.m. every day.

We have English lessons on Mondays.

2 *to express permanent states*

Cambridge is an ancient city.

My friend lives in Scotland.

3 *to express emotions and feelings*

I like ice-cream.

We love English!

Present continuous

1 *to express present actions*

My mum is watching TV (now).

Look! Those kids are having a party.

**7 Copy and complete Mike's story.
Use the present simple and the present continuous.**

Hi! I'm Mike. I (**1** live) in London. It's eight o'clock in the morning. My family and I (**2** have) breakfast at the moment.

Now it's ten o'clock. My sister (**3** talk) to my cousins. I (**4** have) two cousins. They usually (**5** live) in Canada. But they (**6** visit) London at the moment. They sometimes (**7** stay) with us, in our flat. Our cousins (**8** like) London a lot.

It's three o'clock in the afternoon and we (**9** visit) the Tower of London at the moment. We (**10** look) at the crown jewels, and my cousins (**11** take) millions of photos. They (**12** want) to take the crown jewels to Canada. They're crazy!

Study skills

Learning abbreviations

8 Ask and answer about abbreviations.

You What's the abbreviation for 'north'?

Partner The abbreviation for 'north'? It's the letter 'N'.

south east Wednesday Friday
April October *You choose!*

8c Vocabulary

The environment

1 Listen and repeat the words and expressions. 🎧4

2 Answer the questions about your environment.

1 In which country do you live?
2 Which season is it at the moment?
3 Is the weather hot and sunny today?
4 Is it windy today?
5 Do you live near any mountains?
6 Do you live near a river?
7 Is there a lot of traffic where you live?
8 Is there any air pollution where you live?

3 Listen to two conversations. Which two photographs are they talking about? 🎧5

1 photograph ......
2 photograph ......

4 Write a short description of the other photograph in Exercise 3.

English across the curriculum

Environmental studies

1 **Some young people are studying English in Cambridge, England. Read the extracts from their project.**

Cambridge and its environment

Introduction

We come from many different countries in the world. We are studying English in Cambridge. Cambridge is in the east of England. It is a small city. The population is about a hundred thousand.

The city

Cambridge is an ancient city. It is famous because it has a very good university. The main industries in Cambridge are tourism and agriculture. There are also a lot of English language schools in the city.

The environment

The land near Cambridge is flat. There are no hills or mountains! The climate is warm in the summer and cold in the winter. It rains a lot. Sometimes, there is a lot of traffic. And there is usually some air pollution, especially in the centre of the city.

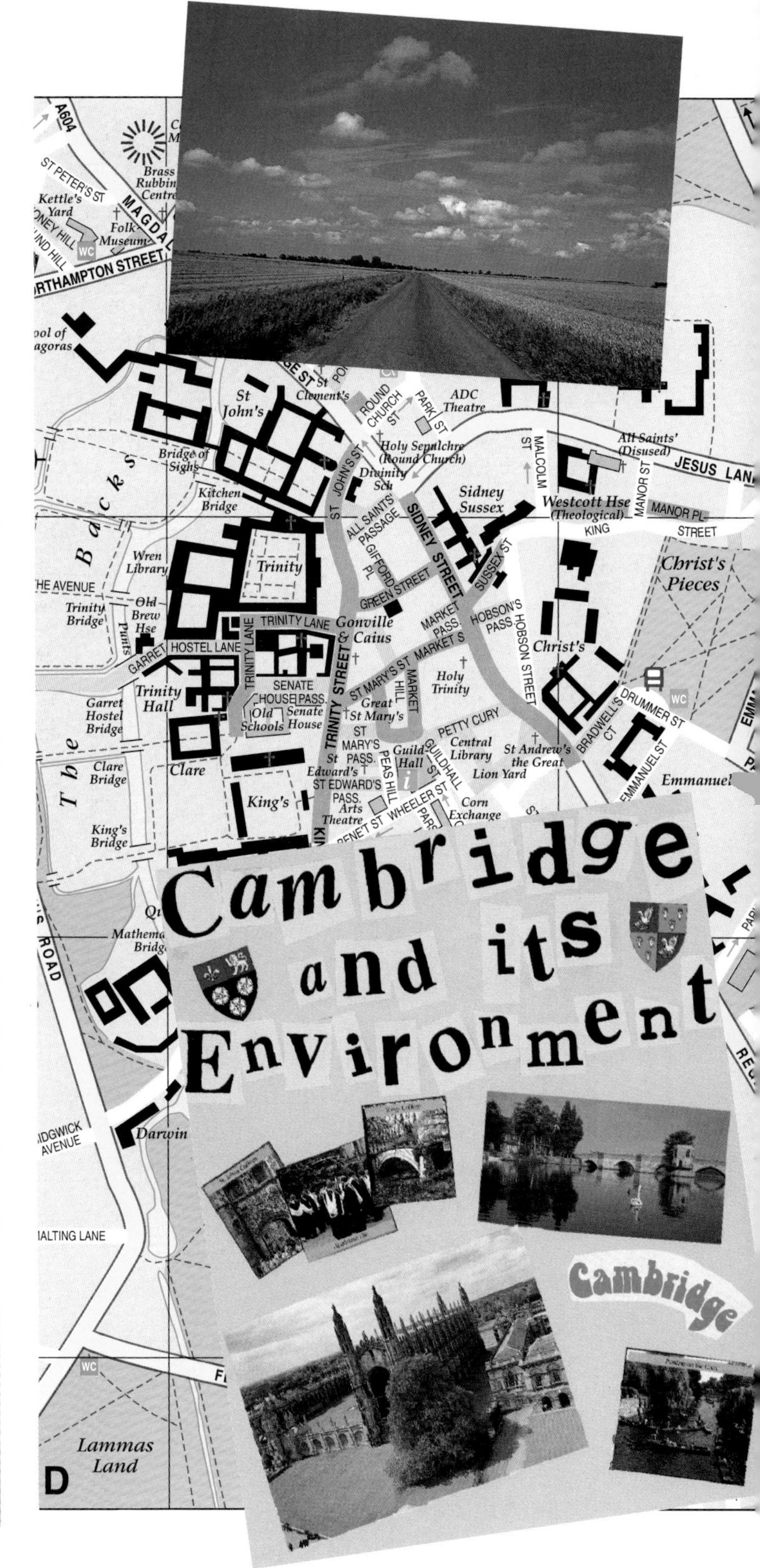

2 **Complete the notes about the students' project.**

Introduction		The city		The environment	
Name	Cambridge	Ancient or modern?	......	The land	......
Type of place	city	Why famous?	......	The climate	......
Size	small	Industries	......	The air	......
Location	......				
Population	......				

3 **In groups, write about your town or city. Write three paragraphs, like those in the text about Cambridge.**

8d

Skills work

Listening

1 Listen to Sergeant Daley. He is in his police car. He is using the radio. Answer the questions. 🎧 6

1 Where is Sergeant Daley?
  a) In Oxford Road.
  b) In Oxford Street.
  c) In Oxford Avenue.

2 What is he doing?
  a) He's looking at a shop.
  b) He's waiting for another police officer.
  c) He's looking at a house.

3 Why?
  a) He's looking for a criminal.
  b) He's lost.
  c) There is a problem with the car.

4 Who are the two men?
  a) Two policemen.
  b) Two criminals.
  c) Sergeant Daley's friends.

5 What are they carrying?
  a) A video.
  b) A television.
  c) Some money.

Writing

2 You receive the phone call from Sergeant Daley. Write his message. Begin:

There is a message from Sergeant Daley. He is in ......

Speaking

3 Find the answers to Sergeant Daley's questions. Then practise the dialogue with your partner.

1 What's your name?
2 Where do you live?
3 What are you doing here?
4 What have you got in your bag?
5 Are they your cassettes?
6 Can you prove it?

I'm going home.	In Oxford Avenue.
Martin White.	Some cassettes.
Well, no, I can't.	Yes, of course they are!

4 Write a dialogue between Sergeant Daley and another person. Use the same questions but different answers.

Progress Diary 8

Grammar

1 Write questions, in the present continuous tense. Then write short answers.

Nick / play / football / at the moment?

Q ......

A (*affirmative*) ......

(*negative*) ......

Sara and Gary / do / their homework / now?

Q ......

A (*affirmative*) ......

(*negative*) ......

2 Complete the questions. Use *What? When? Where? Who?*

...... does the summer holiday start?

...... do you eat for breakfast?

...... do you go for your holidays?

...... is on the phone?

Vocabulary

3 Name the different kinds of weather.

Communication

4 Imagine you are on the phone to a friend. Complete your questions.

Q What ......? **A** I'm doing my homework.

Q ....? **A** My mum? She's watching TV.

Q ......? **A** My brothers? They're reading.

5 Write sentences about your daily routine. Use *often, sometimes, hardly ever, never.*

Pronunciation

6 Complete the table. Use *climate, river, sun, love.*

short vowel /ʌ/	weak vowel /ə/
sun	......
......	......

My progress

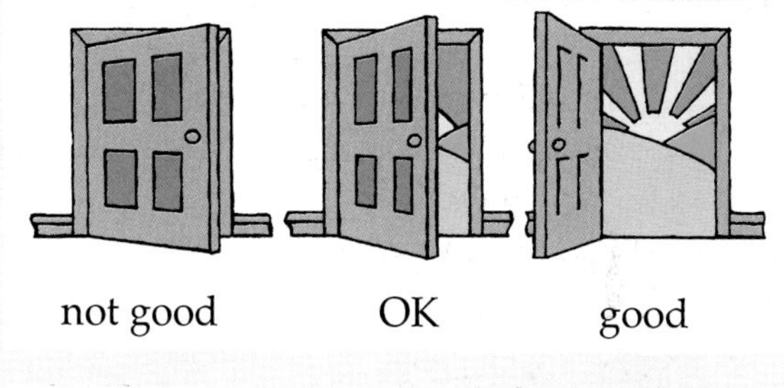

not good   OK   good

In unit 8   I like ......   I don't like ......

9a GARY'S PARTY

1

THINGS TO DO FOR THE PARTY

This week
Wed Write the invitations
Thur Send the invitations
Sat Phone Ana and Petros

Next week
Tue Organize the disco
Thur Buy food and drink
Sat Open my presents

Dear Sara

I'M HAVING A PARTY!

Day and Date Saturday, 20 May
Time 8 p.m.– 12 midnight
Place My house

Gary

1. Today is Wednesday, 10 May. It is Gary's birthday next week.This evening, he is planning his party. At the moment, he is writing some invitations.

2. It's now 10 p.m. Gary is talking to Nick on the phone.

Gary I'm having a party next week.
Nick Great! Are you inviting Sara?
Gary Yes, of course I am. I'm sending the invitations tomorrow.

3. It is Thursday, 18 May. Sara, Ramesh and Nick are at the Sports Centre.

Sara Gary's having a party on Saturday. Are you going, Ramesh?
Ramesh Yes, I am.
Nick (thinks) Oh no! Ramesh's going to Gary's party!

4. Today is Gary's birthday. Nick is talking to Ana in the cassette shop.

Nick What are you doing this evening?
Ana Er, I don't know. Why?
Nick It's Gary's birthday today. He's having a party tonight. Can you come?
Ana I'm sorry, Nick. I am going to the party, but with Petros.
Nick Oh, OK.

Comprehension

1 Answer the questions about Gary's plans. Give the day and the date.

When is Gary buying the food and drink?

On Thursday, 18 May.

1 When is he organizing the disco?

2 When is he phoning Ana and Petros?

3 When is he sending the invitations?

4 When is he opening his presents?

2 Copy and complete the dialogue in your notebook.

Tina When's your birthday, Gary?

Gary On Saturday.

Tina Are you having a party?

Gary ......

Tina What time does the party start?

Gary ......

Tina What time does it finish?

Gary ......

Tina Where are you having the party?

Gary ......

Communication

Talking about future arrangements

3 Listen and repeat. 2

Ramesh What are you doing on Saturday afternoon?

Sara I'm playing basketball.

Ramesh Are you doing your homework on Sunday morning?

Sara Yes, I am.

Ramesh Are you going to the cinema on Sunday evening?

Sara No, I'm not. I'm watching TV then.

4 Plan your weekend activities and complete your diary. Then ask and answer, like Ramesh and Sara.

Saturday	
morning	
afternoon	
evening	
Sunday	
morning	
afternoon	
evening	

You choose!

Pronunciation

Syllables

5 Listen and repeat. 3

1 syllable	2 syllables
this	birth.day
next	par.ty
week	wri.ting
3 syllables	**4 syllables**
Sa.tur.day	in.vi.ta.tions
or.ga.nize	
in.vi.ting	

Listen, repeat and write. How many syllables are there in each word?

1 disco **2** centre **3** Spain

4 Wednesday **5** Greece **6** hamburger

9b Grammar

The present continuous tense (present and future meanings)

1 Compare the two meanings.

Meaning A

These sentences refer to actions *in the present*.

Linda is writing invitations at the moment.

Darren is helping her.

Meaning B

These sentences refer to actions *in the future*.

Linda is phoning Disco Mania on Wednesday.

On Thursday, Darren is buying the food and drink.

Plan for the party

Wed L phone Disco Mania
Thu D buy food and drink
Fri L D phone friends about the party
Sat The party!

2 Which sentences refer to the present? Which sentences refer to the future?

Linda is buying the drinks on Saturday morning.

The future.

1. Darren is helping Linda at the moment.
2. Linda and her friends are doing an exam on Friday.
3. Darren isn't playing football now.
4. Are you going to Linda's party on Saturday?
5. Linda's parents are not going to her party at the weekend!

3 Write five sentences about what you and your friends are *not* doing now.

I'm not listening to music at the moment.

4 Write five sentences about what you and your friends are doing tomorrow.

We're doing a test tomorrow.

Learn this!

Prepositions of time

at nine o'clock	**in** the morning(s)
at the weekend	**in** the afternoon(s)
on Saturday(s)	**in** the evening(s)
on Monday morning	**in** June
on 4 May	**in** the winter

5 **Copy and complete the paragraph about Barry. Use *at, on, in*.**

Barry is fifteen years old. He is a student. He is also a 'paper boy'. He delivers newspapers to houses near his home.

Barry starts work at half past six. He delivers papers every day of the week, from Monday to Saturday, but not (**1**) ... Sundays. He works (**2**) ... the mornings before school, and (**3**) ... the afternoons after school. He usually finishes work (**4**) ... six o'clock. He always does his homework (**5**) ... the evenings.

Barry says, '(**6**) ... the summer, the job is OK, but (**7**) ... December and January, the weather is very cold! I like this job. I get a lot of exercise, and the money is good. I'm saving my money in the bank at the moment. (**8**) ... August, I'm having a holiday in Spain.'

6 **Study the word order.**

Now write the words in the correct order.

don't have / on Sundays. / English students / lessons

English students don't have lessons on Sundays.

1 do / in the evening. / They / their homework
2 their exams / have / British students / in June.
3 at the weekend. / have / Many teenagers / parties
4 I / the car / tomorrow morning. / 'm cleaning
5 in August. / a holiday in England / is having / My cousin
6 our house / My grandparents / are visiting / on Sunday afternoon.

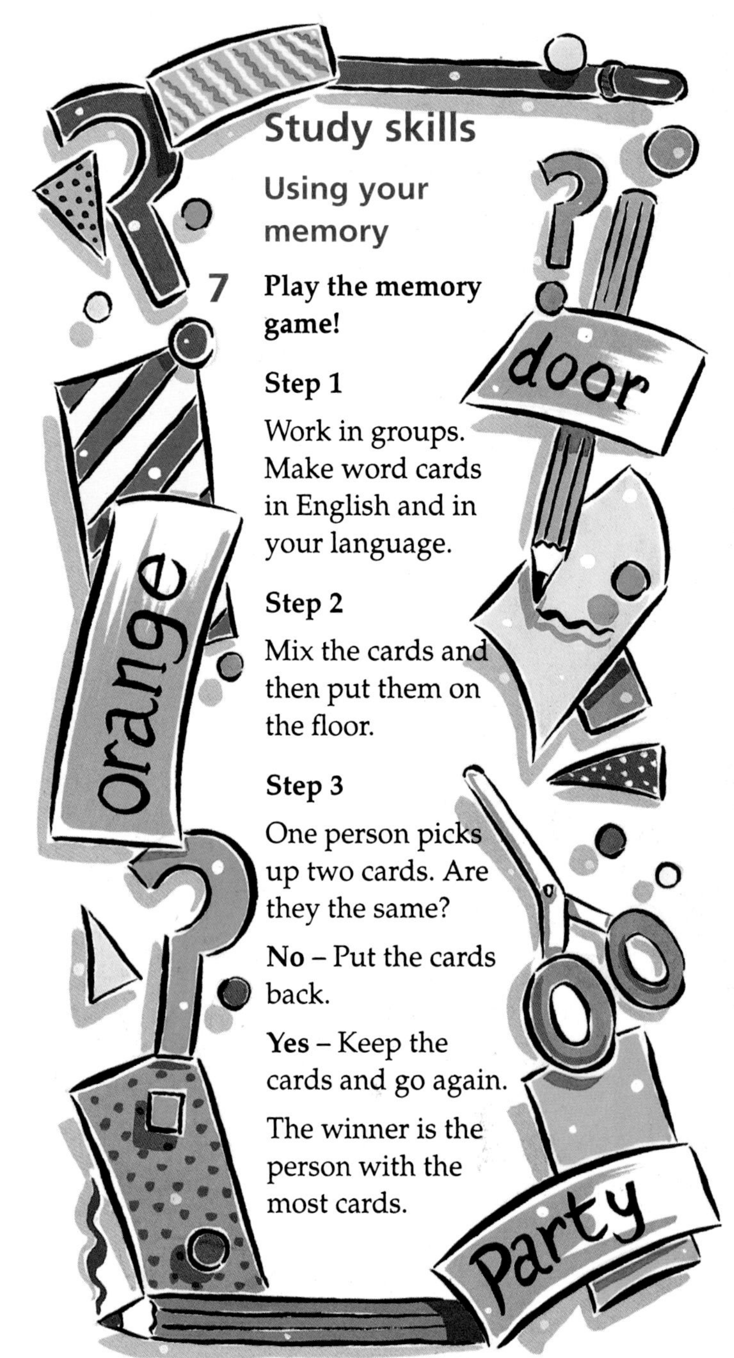

Study skills

Using your memory

7 **Play the memory game!**

Step 1

Work in groups. Make word cards in English and in your language.

Step 2

Mix the cards and then put them on the floor.

Step 3

One person picks up two cards. Are they the same?

No – Put the cards back.

Yes – Keep the cards and go again.

The winner is the person with the most cards.

9c Vocabulary

Objects and materials

1 **Match the objects and the materials. Choose from *cotton, glass, leather, metal, paper, plastic, rubber, wood, wool.* Then listen and check your answers.** 4

2 **Listen and repeat. Then ask and answer about things in the picture.** 5

You What's this called?
Partner It's a guitar.
You What is it made of?
Partner It's made of metal and wood.
You What are these called?
Partner They're bottles.
You What are they made of?
Partner They're made of glass.

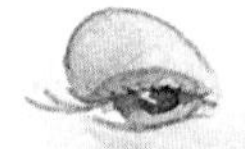
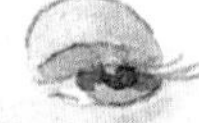

3 **Look around you! Can you name:**

one thing made of paper
two things made of metal
three things made of plastic
four things made of wood

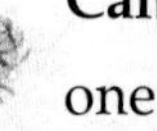

English across the curriculum

Music

pop music

1 Listen and name each person's favourite kind of music. 🎧6

Will *pop music*

1 Angela ......

2 Martin ......

3 Fatima ......

rock music

2 Ask and answer.

You What's your favourite kind of music?

Partner ......

You Who's your favourite singer?

Partner ......

You Who's your favourite group?

Partner ......

folk music

3 Listen to Jenny and Keith. Copy and complete the table.
✔ = likes, ✘ = doesn't like 🎧7

classical music

	Jenny	Keith
listening to pop music	✘	✔
dancing to pop music		
listening to opera		
playing classical music		
listening to jazz		

jazz

4 Ask three students about their likes and dislikes.

Do you like	dancing to listening to playing	pop music? rock music? classical music? folk music? Greek, American, ... music? jazz?	Yes, I do. No, I don't.

5 Write six true sentences.

I like reading about pop music.

My friend ... doesn't like listening to classical music.

My friends ... and ... like dancing to pop music.

Learn this!
I like pop music.
I like listen**ing** to pop music.

9d Skills work

Speaking

1 Ask and answer.

Do you play a musical instrument?

Can you sing?

Are you musical?

Reading

2 Read about Miss Newman's music group in Year 10. Then answer the questions in numbers and words.

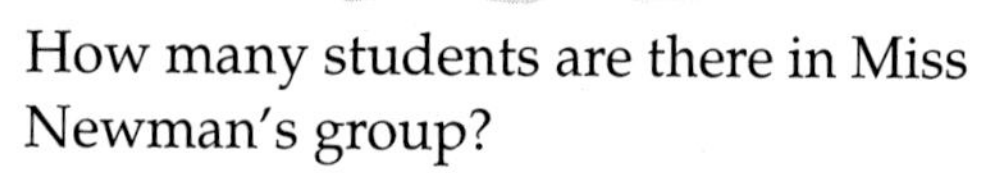

There are twenty-three students in Miss Newman's music group. All of the students in the group like music very much, and they enjoy Miss Newman's lessons a lot.

Fifteen of the students are good singers. Ten of them are in the school choir. There is a choir practice every week, on Wednesday evening. The choir can sing songs in different languages, including English, French, German and Spanish.

Some students in Miss Newman's group can play a musical instrument. Four can play the flute, two can play the clarinet and one can play the cello. Another student in the group can play the piano, and one can play the saxophone. Four of the students are very good players, and they are in the school orchestra.

All the students in the group are very musical, but none of them can play the guitar. So, next week, Miss Newman is starting guitar lessons. And, next month, she is teaching them about the history of rock music!

How many students are there in Miss Newman's group?

23 – twenty-three

1. How many like music?
2. How many do **not** sing in the school choir?
3. How many can play a musical instrument?
4. How many do **not** play in the school orchestra?
5. How many can play the guitar?

Listening

3 Listen to Mr Green and his class and answer the questions. 8

1. How many students are there in Mr Green's class?
2. How many like pop music?
3. How many play a musical instrument?
4. How many can sing?
5. How many like classical music?
6. How many like opera?

> **Learn this!**
> Expressions of quantity
> <u>All</u> (<u>of</u>) the students like music.
> <u>None of</u> the students can play the guitar.

Progress Diary 9

Grammar

1 Does each sentence mean present time or future time?

Dad's cleaning the car on Saturday.

I'm helping my friend at the moment.

Look! Dad's cleaning the car.

'What's Sue doing now?' 'She's doing a test.'

I'm helping my friend tonight.

We're doing a test tomorrow.

2 Complete the sentences. Use *in, on, at*.

She's going to England …… 9 August.

She's having a holiday …… August.

Her plane is leaving …… midnight.

3 Translate.

All (of) the students are here.

None of the students are here.

Vocabulary

4 Name three classroom objects and what they are made of.

table – wood …… ……

Name three kinds of music.

rock …… ……

Name three musical instruments.

piano …… ……

Communication

5 Write questions and answers.

you / morning? / are / tomorrow / doing / What

the / party / Are / having / at / weekend? / a / you

Pronunciation

6 How many syllables are there in these words?

1 finishes **2** future **3** student **4** play

My progress

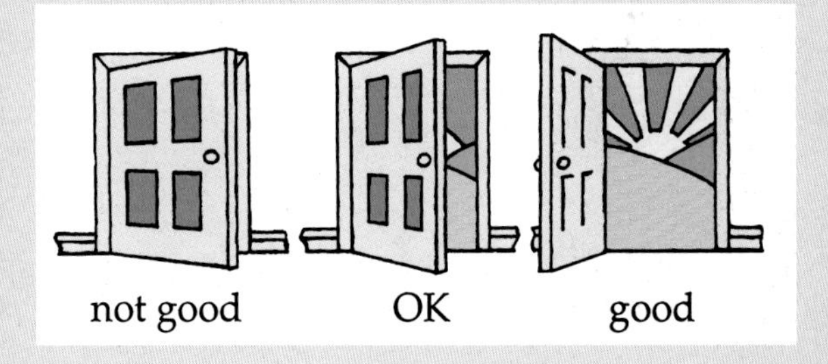

In unit 9 I like …… I don't like ……

I like jazz!

Listen and repeat. 9

10a GOOD NEWS!

1

1 Today is the last day of Nick's exams.

Nick Tracy. Be quiet! I must study for my science exam.

Tracy What? I can't hear you!

Mum Tracy. Turn your radio off. You mustn't make a lot of noise. Nick's very nervous about his exam.

2 Nick's mum is reading a letter from her brother.

Mum Good news! Your Uncle Dave's going to visit us.

285 Sunset Road
Harbour View
Sydney
Australia
Saturday, 3 June

Dear Sue,

Good news! The university is sending me to England. We're flying to London on Sunday 15 July and we're arriving the next day at 3 p.m.

First, I'm spending two weeks at the Science Museum in London. June and the twins are going to visit some friends in Oxford. Then we're all going to spend a week in Brighton. In the second week of August, we're going to drive to Scotland. We're going to stay with Mum and Dad. In September, we're going to travel round Europe by car.

Are you going to be in London in July? Can we stay with you? I hope so!

See you soon,

Dave

PS How are Nick and Tracy? Can we take them to Scotland?

3 **Nick** Great! Are Mark and Cathie coming, too?

Mum Yes, they are. And Auntie June. They want to take you and Tracy to Scotland.

4 **Nick** Great! I must go now. I mustn't miss the bus today.

Tracy Oh, Nick. Good luck with your exam!

Comprehension

1 Answer the questions.

What **must** Nick do before breakfast?

He must study for his science exam.

1 What **must** Tracy do this morning?
2 What **must** Tracy **not** do this morning?
3 What **must** Nick **not** do today?

2 Answer the questions.

Who is going to spend two weeks at the Science Museum in London?

Tracy's uncle, Dave Macintosh.

1 **Who** are going to visit some friends in Oxford?
2 **When** are Dave and his family going to drive to Scotland?
3 **Who** are they going to stay with in Scotland?
4 **When** are they going to travel round Europe?
5 **How** are they going to travel round Europe?
6 **When** are Dave and his family arriving in London?

Day ...... Date ...... Time ......

Numbers

3 Change the numbers into words.

two hundred and eighty-five

one thousand, three hundred and seventy-six

Communication

Plans and intentions

4 Listen and repeat the dialogue. 2

Philip Are you going to visit Greece?

Cathie Yes, I am.

Philip Are you going to visit Sweden?

Cathie No, I'm not.

5 Which three countries are you going to visit? Choose, then ask and answer, like Philip and Cathie.

Pronunciation

Syllables and word stress

6 Listen and repeat. 3

stress the *first* syllable
'break.fast 'read.ing

stress the *second* syllable
to.'day e.'xam

stress the *third* syllable
u.ni.'ver.si.ty

Listen, repeat and write. Which syllable must you stress? The first, second, or third?

1 four.teen 2 Au.gust 3 mu.se.um
4 Sep.tem.ber 5 for.ty 6 Eu.ro.pe.an

10b Grammar

going to (future plans and intentions)

1 Look at the pictures and answer the questions.

1. Who's going to have a holiday in Spain?
2. Who's going to travel by car?
3. Who's going to travel by plane?

2 Now copy and complete the sentences in your notebook. Use *is going to, isn't going to, are going to, aren't going to.*

Sue and her family ...... have a holiday in Greece.

Sue and her family aren't going to have a holiday in Greece.

1. Sue ...... have a holiday with her family.
2. Linda and Darren ...... visit Spain.
3. Linda and Darren ...... travel by car.
4. Mike ...... have his holiday in France.
5. Mike and his family ...... have a sailing holiday.
6. Sue, Darren, Linda and Mike ...... have their holidays in England!

going to (predictions)

3 What's going to happen? Use *have an accident, rain, sit on the sandwiches.*

1. Careful, Mum! You're going to ......
2. Mike! Your dad's going to ......
3. Hurry up! It's going to ......

Personal pronouns

4 **Copy and complete the table. Use *them, me, you, us, her, you, it, him.***

subject	object
I	me
you	

5 **Complete Mrs Johnson's phone call to her father in Scotland. Use the correct object pronouns.**

Hello, Dad! It's good to hear you.

Good news. Dave' s coming to Britain. We're going to meet (**1**) ...... at the airport on July the sixteenth. June and the kids are coming too. We're going to take (**2**) ...... to Oxford. Cathie also wants to buy some new clothes, so I'm going to take (**3**) ...... shopping in London.

Nick and Tracy are fine. Dave's going to take (**4**) ...... to Scotland. So all your grandchildren are going to see (**5**) ...... this summer.

When are you going to visit (**6**) ...... here in London? You and Mum are always welcome!

I must go now. Jim's taking (**7**) ...... to a restaurant this evening. The kids are staying at home. Their exams are tomorrow.

I'm writing you a letter and I'm going to send (**8**) ...... tomorrow.

Bye!

Now listen and check your answers. 4

must (obligation) and *mustn't* (prohibition)

6 **Complete the sentences. Use *must* or *mustn't*.**

1 You ...... go to the dentist.

2 You ...... eat chocolates.

3 You ...... watch TV.

4 You ...... study for your exams.

Study skills

Listening for detail

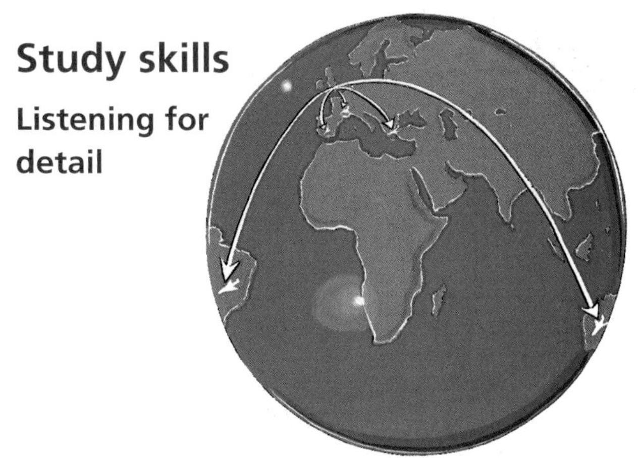

7 **Listen to the pilot and choose the correct number.** 5

How far is Paris from London?

a) 430 km **b)** (340 km) **c)** 314 km

1 How far is Madrid from London?

a) 1,240 km **b)** 1,420 km **c)** 1,214 km

2 How far is Athens from London?

a) 2,614 km **b)** 2,460 km **c)** 2,416 km

3 How far is Rio de Janeiro from London?

a) 9,215 km **b)** 9,250 km **c)** 9,255 km

4 How far is Sydney from London?

a) 17,009 km **b)** 17,090 km **c)** 17,019 km

10c Vocabulary

Time

1 Match each word with its definition.

	Time words		Definitions
1	one minute	a)	twenty-four hours
2	one hour	b)	ten years
3	one day	c)	four to five weeks
4	one week	d)	twelve months
5	one month	e)	a hundred years
6	one year	f)	seven days
7	one decade	g)	sixty minutes
8	one century	h)	sixty seconds
9	one millennium	i)	a thousand years

2 Write five of your answers to exercise 1 in sentences in your notebook.

One minute equals sixty seconds.

Now listen and check your answers. 6

3 Study the example. Then answer the questions.

a) How many seconds are there in a minute?

There are sixty (60) seconds in a minute.

b) How many minutes are there in an hour?

There are sixty minutes in an hour.

c) So, how many seconds are there in an hour?

There are three thousand, six hundred (3,600) seconds in an hour.

1 **a)** How many hours are there in a day?
b) How many days are there in a week?
c) So, how many hours are there in a week?

2 **a)** How many months are there in a year?
b) How many years are there in a decade?
c) So, how many months are there in a decade?

3 **a)** How many decades are there in a century?
b) How many centuries are there in a millennium?
c) So, how many decades are there in a millennium?

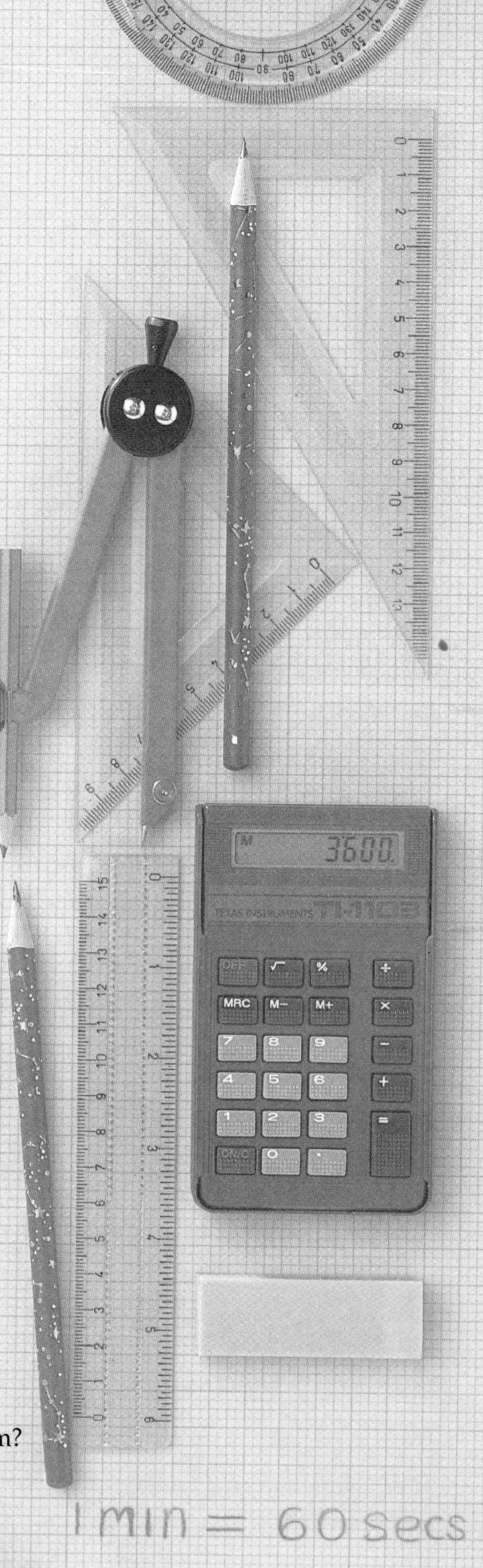

English across the curriculum

Science: the solar system

Space

1 **Match the numbers and planets. Use *Earth, Jupiter, Mars, Mercury, Neptune, Pluto, Saturn, Uranus, Venus*. Then listen and check your answers.** 7

2 **Listen again and choose the correct answer.**

1 Mercury is very cold/hot/wet at night.
2 Venus has got a lot of rings/moons/clouds around it.
3 There isn't any water/light/rock on Mars.
4 Saturn and Uranus are made of rock/gas/water.
5 Neptune has got a lot of clouds/moons/hills.
6 Pluto is very hot/cold/wet.

3 **Find the ten 'space' words.**

A	R	S	O	M	O	O	N	E
R	S	A	T	U	P	S	T	A
J	U	T	E	R	L	L	A	R
U	R	U	E	U	U	V	A	T
P	L	R	A	R	T	R	E	H
I	M	N	R	A	O	O	N	N
T	O	A	T	N	R	I	N	G
E	O	P	R	U	P	L	D	T
R	I	N	T	S	T	A	R	S

10d Skills work

Reading

1 **Read the table. Now answer the questions. Write the answers in words.**

Planet Chart

Planet	How big across	How far from the sun	How many moons	How many rings
Mercury	4,850 km	59 million km	none	none
Venus	12,140 km	108 million km	none	none
Earth	12,756 km	150 million km	1	none
Mars	6,790 km	228 million km	2	none
Jupiter	142,600 km	778 million km	at least 16	2
Saturn	120,200 km	1,427 million km	at least 17	many
Uranus	49,000 km	2,870 million km	at least 15	10
Neptune	50,000 km	4,497 million km	8	4
Pluto	about 3,000 km	5,900 million km	1	none

How far is Mars from the sun?

Two hundred and twenty-eight million kilometres.

1 How far is Mercury from the sun?
2 How many moons does Neptune have?
3 How big is the planet Saturn?
4 How many rings does Venus have?
5 How many moons does Uranus have?
6 How big is the Earth?

Speaking

2 **Ask and answer about the planets.**

You How big is the planet Mars?
Partner It's ...... kilometres across.
You How far is Venus from the sun?
Partner One hundred and eight million kilometres.

Writing

3 **First read the paragraph. What is the name of this planet?**

THIS PLANET is twelve thousand, one hundred and forty kilometres across. It is one hundred and eight million kilometres from the sun. It has no moon and no rings.

4 **Now write a similar paragraph about another planet. Read your description to the class. Can they guess which planet it is?**

Progress Diary 10

Grammar

1 Make the sentence negative.

He's going to have a party at the weekend.

Make the sentence interrogative.

They're going to have a holiday in August.

2 Copy and complete the table of personal pronouns.

subject	I	you	she	......
object	me	you	......	

Vocabulary

3 Write the list of time words in their correct order.

century day decade hour minute month second week year

1 second 2 minute 3 ......

Communication

4 Write true answers to these questions.

a) future arrangements (*present continuous*)

What are you doing tomorrow evening?

I'm ......

b) future plans and intentions (*going to*)

What are you going to do at the weekend?

I'm ......

5 Answer the questions about predictions.

Who's going to win the tennis game?
Who's going to lose the tennis game?

Alice 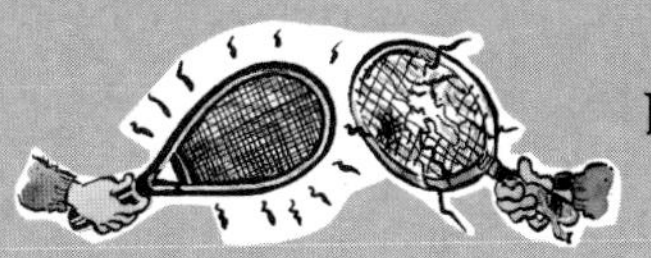 Brian

6 Complete the sentences. Use *must* or *mustn't*.

I've got an exam tomorrow. I ...... study and I ...... watch TV tonight.
This exam is important and I ...... pass.

Pronunciation

7 Practise the stress on different syllables.

'A.pril 'mor.ning 'pho.to
Sep.'tember af.ter.'noon
pho.'to.gra.phy

My progress

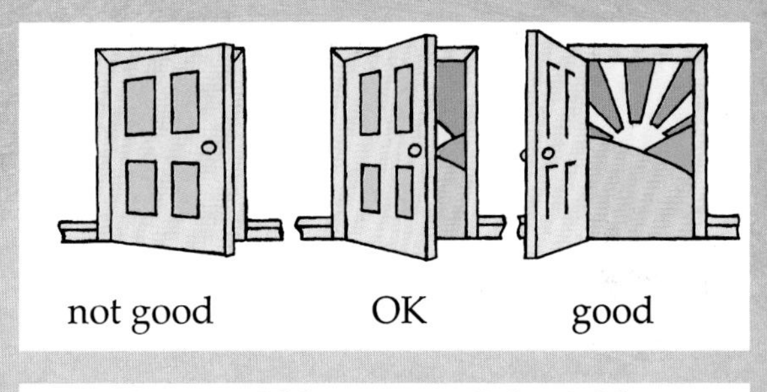

not good OK good

In unit 10 I like ...... I don't like ......

What are we going to do?

Listen and complete the words of the song. 8

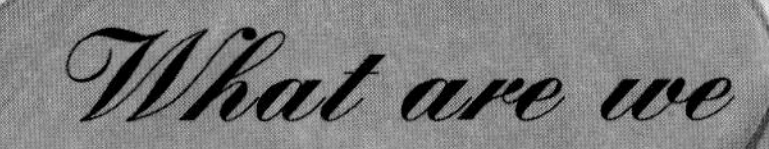

I'm losing (1) ......
She's leaving (2) ......
What am I going to do?
I'm waiting here
She's leaving (3) ......
What am I going to do?

I'm losing (4) ......
He's leaving (5)......
What am I going to do?
I'm waiting here
He's leaving (6) ......
What am I going to do?

What are we going to do, my love? What are we going to do?
We're waiting here, Love's leaving (7) ......
What are we going to do?

11a WAS THAT THE MONSTER?

1

Nick and Tracy are on holiday in Scotland, with Uncle Dave and his family. They are all staying with Nick's grandparents, Mr and Mrs Macintosh.

2 Thursday, 10 August

Dave Look! Was that the monster?

Tracy Where? I can't see it.

Nick Don't be silly, Tracy. That wasn't the monster. It was a joke!

3 Monday, 14 August

Dave Was the castle interesting?

Cathie Yes, it was great.

Dave Were those books expensive, Cathie?

Cathie No, they weren't, Dad. They were cheap.

Friday
Dear Gary
I was at Loch Ness yesterday, but the monster wasn't! The weather is OK today. But yesterday it was cold and windy.
See you soon, Nick

Gary Slade
29, Mill Street
London
NW10 8JF
England

4

June How much time have we got, Dave?

Dave Oh, no, June! How many souvenirs are you going to buy?

Tuesday
Dear Mum and Dad
Yesterday Cathie and I were in Edinburgh. The castle was very interesting. Auntie June has got millions of souvenirs.
Love Tracy

Mum and Dad
85, Palace Road
London
NW10 12NK
England

Comprehension

1 **Copy and complete Cathie's sentences about her holiday. Use *I, My books, The Loch Ness monster, My grandparents, Nick's friend Gary, The weather, My cousin Tracy and I***

...... was at Loch Ness on Thursday.

I was at Loch Ness on Thursday.

1 ...... wasn't at Loch Ness on Thursday.

2 ...... was cold at Loch Ness.

3 ...... wasn't with us in Scotland.

4 ...... were in Edinburgh on Monday.

5 ...... weren't with us at Edinburgh Castle.

6 ...... weren't expensive.

Communication

Talking about the past

2 **Listen and repeat.** 2

Nick Where were you on Thursday, Ana?

Ana I was at school.

Nick Where were you on Sunday evening?

Ana I was at the cinema.

Ana Were you in Scotland last week, Nick?

Nick Yes, I was.

Ana Were you at Loch Ness on Sunday?

Nick No, I wasn't. I was at my grandma's house.

3 **Where were you last week? Copy and complete *your* diary. Then ask and answer like Nick and Ana.**

DIARY
Fri
morning
afternoon
Sat
morning
afternoon
Sun
morning
afternoon

at the cinema

at a friend's house

You choose!

Pronunciation

Stress and rhythm

4 **Listen and repeat.** 3

'That 'wasn't the 'monster.

'It was a 'joke.

'Were those 'books ex'pensive?

'No, they 'weren't, 'Dad! They were 'cheap.

Listen and repeat. Which words and syllables are stressed?

Nick and Tracy live in London.

Nick and Tracy don't live in Scotland.

11b Grammar

The past simple tense of the verb *be*

1 Study the past simple tense of the verb *be*.

affirmative	negative	interrogative		
	full forms/short forms	*questions*	*short answers*	
I **was**	I **was not / wasn't**	**Was** I …?	Yes, I **was**.	No, I **wasn't**.
you **were**	you **were not / weren't**	**Were** you …?	Yes, you **were**.	No, you **weren't**.
she / he / it **was**	she / he / it **was not / wasn't**	**Was** she …? / he …? / it …?	Yes, she / he / it **was**.	No, she / he / it **wasn't**.
we / you / they **were**	we / you / they **were not / weren't**	**Were** we …? / you …? / they …?	Yes, we / you / they **were**.	No, we / you / they **weren't**.

2 Darren's cousins Steve and Jane are travel guides. Read about their busy week and answer the questions.

1 Where was Steve on Wednesday?

2 Where was Jane on Monday?

3 Where were Steve and Jane on Tuesday?

4 Where was Steve on Friday?

5 Where were Steve and Jane on Saturday?

3 Complete and answer the questions.

Was Steve in London on Monday?

Yes, he was.

Were Steve and Jane in Lisbon on Wednesday?

No, they weren't.

1 …… Steve and Jane in Paris on Tuesday?

2 …… Jane in London on Friday?

3 …… Steve in Madrid on Thursday?

4 …… Jane in Athens on Wednesday?

5 …… Jane and Steve in London on Saturday?

6 …… Steve in Lisbon on Tuesday?

4 **Complete these sentences to make true statements. Use *was, wasn't, were, weren't.***

I ...... in Wales last year.

I wasn't in Wales last year.

1 I ...... at school yesterday.

2 My friend ...... at home last Friday.

3 My friends ...... in England last summer.

4 My family and I ...... at home last Sunday morning.

5 My mum ...... at work yesterday.

6 My English teacher ...... in America last year.

Countable and uncountable nouns

5 **Revise countable and uncountable nouns. Arrange the nouns into two groups.**

souvenir water cities student
money sugar bread souvenirs
girls city students girl

countable		**uncountable**
singular	*plural*	*singular only*
souvenir	......	money

How much? How many?

6 **Study the questions and answers.**

Q **How many** souvenirs have you got?

A Three.

Q **How much** orange juice have you got?

A Two litres.

Learn this!

How many + countable nouns, plural
How much + uncountable nouns

7 **Copy and complete the questions. Use *How many ...? How much ...?***

Then answer the questions.

1 ...... students are there in your class today?

2 ...... money do you have in your pockets at the moment?

3 ...... brothers and sisters do you have?

4 ...... water do you drink each day?

5 ...... apples do you eat every week?

6 ...... English words do you know?

Study skills

Dates

8 **Change the numbers into words.**

1492 Christopher Columbus lands in America

That was in fourteen ninety-two.

1564 The birth of William Shakespeare

1789 The French Revolution

1969 Neil Armstrong lands on the moon

11c Vocabulary

Souvenirs

1 **Listen and repeat the names of the souvenirs.** 4

2 **Listen to the dialogue. Then practise with a partner.** 5

LONDON SOUVENIRS
RECEIPT

Items	Price each		Sub total
1 sweatshirt	£12.50	=	£12.50
3 pens	70p	=	£2.10
GRAND TOTAL		=	£14.60

Man Hello. What would you like?

Girl I'd like a sweatshirt, please.

Man One sweatshirt. That's twelve pounds fifty, please.

Girl How much are the pens?

Man They're seventy pence each.

Girl OK. Can I have three, please?

Man Right. That's two pounds ten, and twelve pounds fifty for the sweatshirt. Fourteen sixty altogether. And here's a carrier bag.

Girl Thank you very much.

3 **Listen. Complete the receipts for these two customers.** 6

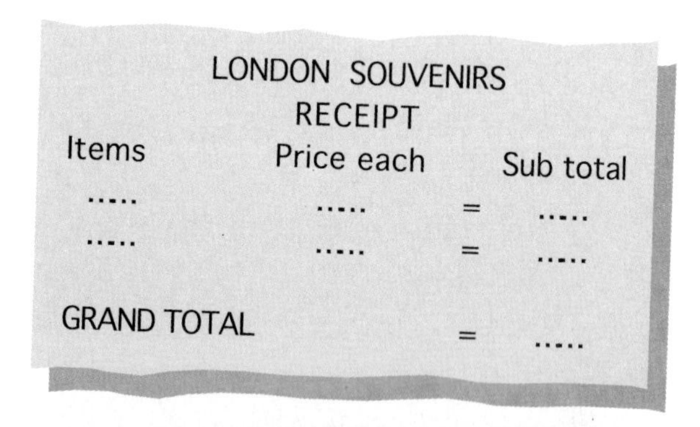

LONDON SOUVENIRS
RECEIPT

Items	Price each		Sub total
.....	.....	=	.....
.....	.....	=	.....
GRAND TOTAL		=	.....

Learn this!

18p = eighteen pence
35p = thirty-five pence
£1 = one pound
£5.22 = five pounds, twenty-two

English across the curriculum

History: legends from different countries

1 **Listen and read about legends.** 7

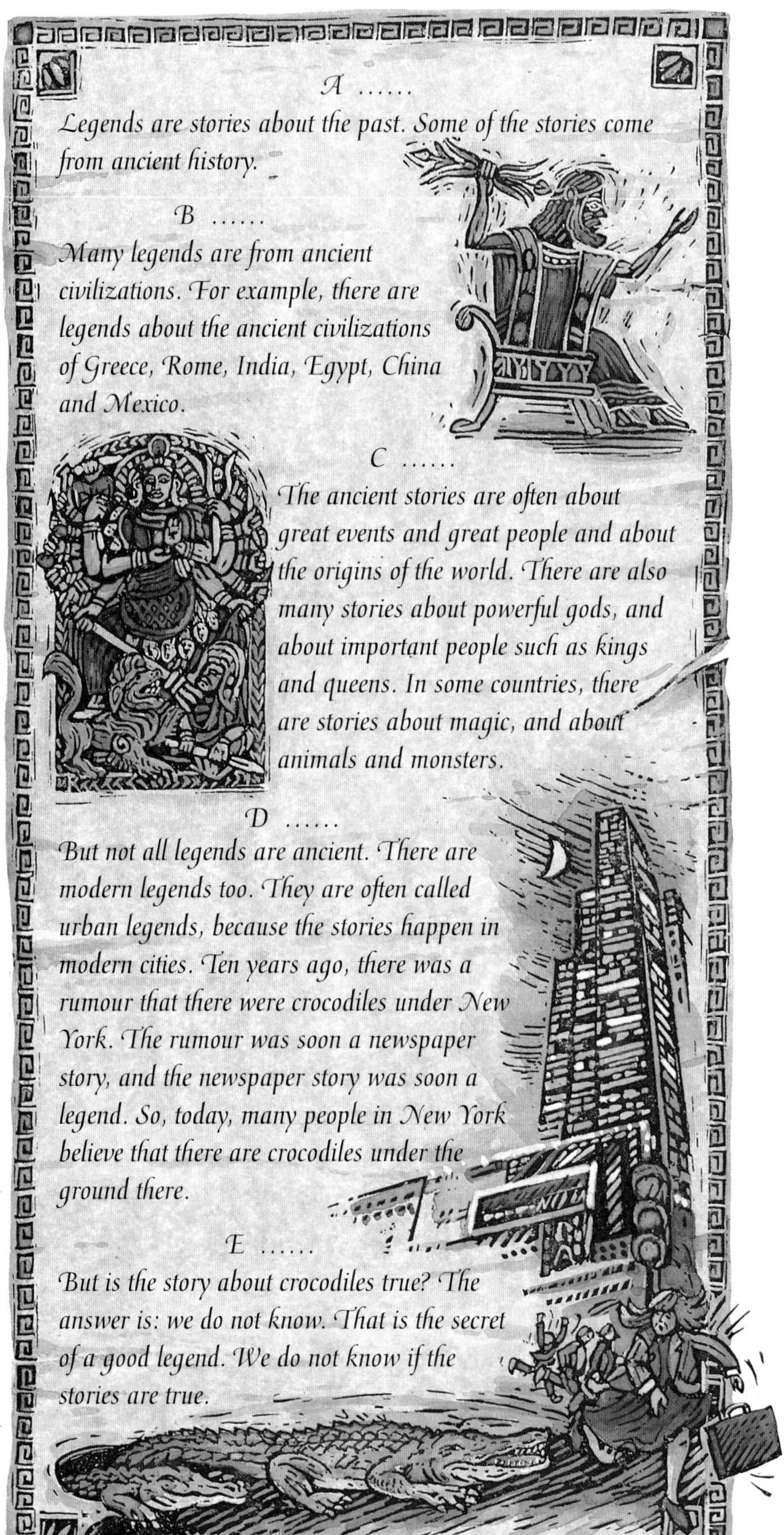

A ......

Legends are stories about the past. Some of the stories come from ancient history.

B ......

Many legends are from ancient civilizations. For example, there are legends about the ancient civilizations of Greece, Rome, India, Egypt, China and Mexico.

C ......

The ancient stories are often about great events and great people and about the origins of the world. There are also many stories about powerful gods, and about important people such as kings and queens. In some countries, there are stories about magic, and about animals and monsters.

D ......

But not all legends are ancient. There are modern legends too. They are often called urban legends, because the stories happen in modern cities. Ten years ago, there was a rumour that there were crocodiles under New York. The rumour was soon a newspaper story, and the newspaper story was soon a legend. So, today, many people in New York believe that there are crocodiles under the ground there.

E ......

But is the story about crocodiles true? The answer is: we do not know. That is the secret of a good legend. We do not know if the stories are true.

2 **Choose the correct heading for each paragraph.**

Examples from different countries

Legends today

Conclusion: An important question

Introduction: Legends – a definition

What are legends about?

3 **What do these words mean? Choose the best answer: a), b) or c).**

1 legend
- **a)** story
- **b)** history
- **c)** person

2 ancient
- **a)** large
- **b)** old
- **c)** important

3 origins
- **a)** beginning
- **b)** end
- **c)** people

4 modern
- **a)** new
- **b)** important
- **c)** different

5 truth
- **a)** fact
- **b)** joke
- **c)** legend

6 believe
- **a)** know
- **b)** say
- **c)** think

11d Skills work

Reading

1 Read about the legend of the Loch Ness monster.

The Loch Ness monster

In Scotland, there is a popular legend about a monster. The monster lives in a lake called Loch Ness, near the town of Inverness. Loch Ness is 32 km long, 5 km wide, and very, very deep. The monster's name is Nessie. People say that she is very big, and that she has got a long neck, like a snake.

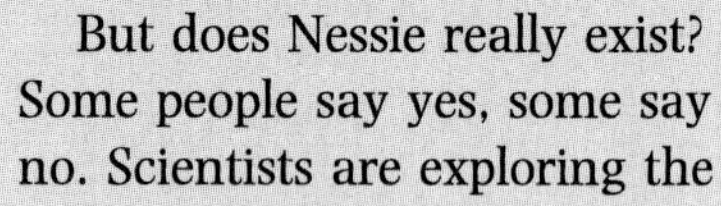

But does Nessie really exist? Some people say yes, some say no. Scientists are exploring the lake with cameras and sound equipment. Sometimes they see something and sometimes they hear something, but they do not understand the mystery of Loch Ness.

The legend of the monster is very famous, and millions of tourists from all over the world come to Loch Ness. Everybody wants to be the first person to see Nessie. Come to Scotland and Loch Ness – that person may be you!

True or false?

Loch Ness is near Edinburgh. *False.*

1 Loch Ness is a very deep lake.
2 Nessie is very small.
3 She has a long neck.
4 Tourists are exploring the lake.
5 They never see anything.
6 A lot of tourists come to Loch Ness.

Listening

2 Listen. Which civilization and legend are they talking about? 8

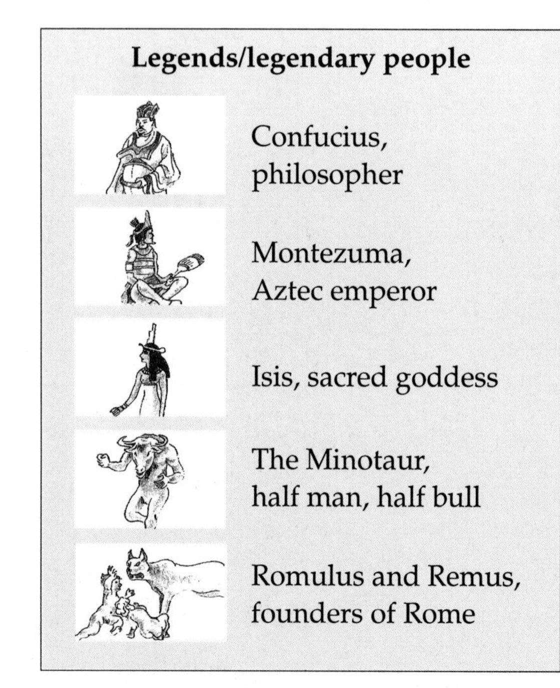

Ancient civilizations	Legends/legendary people
Egyptian	Confucius, philosopher
Greek	Montezuma, Aztec emperor
Roman	Isis, sacred goddess
Mexican	The Minotaur, half man, half bull
Chinese	Romulus and Remus, founders of Rome

	Civilization	Legend
1 Jake	*Mexican*	*Montezuma*
2 Hannah	......	......
3 Maria and Ivan	......	......

Writing

3 Make notes about a legend that you know. Choose an ancient story from your country, or a modern urban legend. Write the events of the story in the present tense and include a picture.

Title *The legend of* ......

The characters ......

Events in the story ......

Speaking

4 Turn your notes into a short talk. Tell your story to the class.

PROGRESS DIARY 11

Grammar

1 Complete the table.

The past simple tense of the verb *be*.

	affirmative	negative	
		full forms	*short forms*
I	was	......	......
she he it	......	......	......
we you they	......	......	......

2 Complete the sentences. Use *How much? How many?*

...... cassettes have you got?
...... Coke have you got?
...... rice have you got?
...... maps have you got?

Vocabulary

3 Name the souvenirs.

Communication

4 Write three true sentences about the past.

Yesterday at 3.00 p.m., I ......
Last Monday, my friend ......
Last year, my friends ......

5 Which question is about *price*? Which question is about *quantity*?

How many would you like?
How much are those pencils?

Pronunciation

6 Practise stress and rhythm.

'My 'cousin is a fan'tastic pho'tographer.
'English is 'easy!

My progress

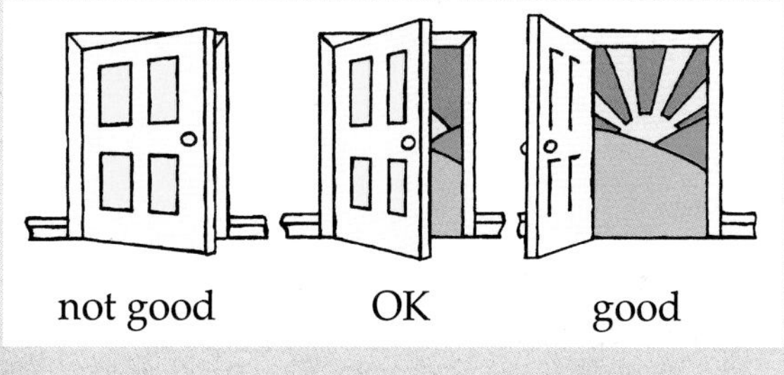

In unit 11 I like ...... I don't like ......

The monster rap!

Listen and repeat. 9

There in the forest
Here in the sea
Is that the monster
We can see?

Hands! Hands!
Look at those hands!
Feet! Feet!
Look at those feet!

Eyes! Eyes!
What a surprise!
Face! Face!
What a disgrace!

We like coffee
We like tea
But we don't like monsters
In the sea!

12a AN INTERNATIONAL EVENING

1

Wembley School of English

✶

Invitation to an International Evening.
We're celebrating the end of our course
with food and wine from many countries.

✶

Saturday 26 August

2
Ana Yesterday was the last day of our English course. We learned a lot from our teachers.
Nick When was your trip to Stratford?
Ana Thursday, the day before yesterday.

3
Nick These photos are great!
Ana Thanks. First, we visited Shakespeare's birthplace. Then we walked round the town. It rained all the time. There were thousands of people there, but I liked it.

4 Later, a group played music and everybody danced.

Comprehension

1 Write the dates for these events.

The students' International Evening.
Saturday, 26 August.

1 The last day of Ana's English course.
2 Ana's flight home.
3 Petros's return to Greece.
4 Ana's trip to Stratford.
5 The first day of Cathie's holiday in France.

2 Complete the puzzle with words from the story.

Across

1 Yuki comes from this country.
4 They help you at school.
8 Cathie lives ...... Australia.
10 Ana visited this place on Thursday.
12 It ...... all the time on Thursday.

Down

2 The capital city of Greece.
3 The plural form of *I*.
4 A day of the week.
5 Nick wants Yuki's ....
6 Ana lives in this country.
7 Ana ...... round Stratford.
9 Stratford isn't a village. It's a ....
11 Mark is going .... France next week.

■	■	■	1 J	2 A	P	A	N	■	■	■
■	3	■	■		■	■	■	■	■	■
4		5					6	■	■	■
	■		■		■	■		■	■	7
	■		■		■	■		■	■	
	■		■		■	■	8		■	
	■		■	■	■	■		■	■	
	■		■	■	■	■	■	9	■	
	■	10	11							
	■	■		■	■	■	■		■	■
■	■	■	■	■	12					

Communication

Conversational English

3 You are in London. You meet someone at an international party. Complete the conversation.

1 **You** Hi! What's your name?
Partner ......
2 **You** Where are you from?
Partner ......
3 **You** How old are you?
Partner ......
4 **You** Is this your first trip to England?
Partner ......
5 **You** How many languages do you speak?
Partner ......
6 **You** Would you like to dance?
Partner ......

Pronunciation

Intonation – falling ↘ and rising ↗

4 Listen and repeat. 2

We learned a lot from our teachers.↘
These photos are great.↘
Are you from Spain?↗
Can I have your address in Japan, Yuki?↗

Dictation. Listen, repeat and write the sentences.

Does the intonation fall ↘ or rise ↗ ?

1 ...... 2 ......
3 ...... 4 ......

12b Grammar

The past simple tense (affirmative)

1 Compare the base form and the past simple form of these verbs.

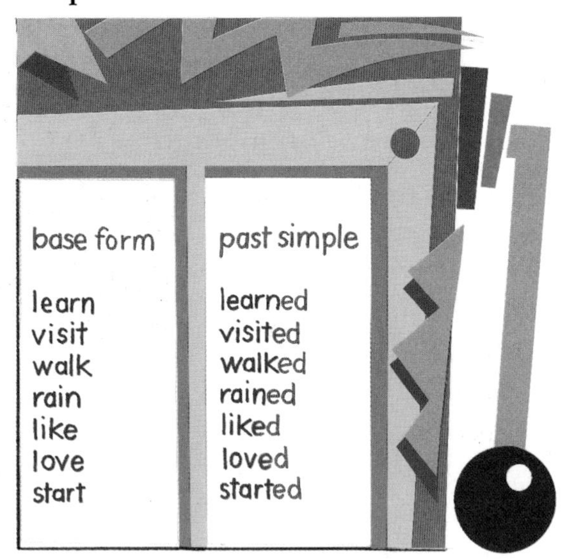

Complete the spelling rule.

The past simple of regular verbs
= base form + ... or ......

2 Copy and complete the table.

base form	*past simple*
celebrate	celebrated
dance	
phone	
enjoy	
play	
walk	
wash	

3 Write each sentence in the past simple tense.

I ...... my mum yesterday (phone)

I phoned my mum yesterday.

1 I ...... TV last night. (watch)
2 My friend ...... the film last night. (like)
3 We ...... our grandparents on Sunday. (visit)
4 We ...... a lot of new words yesterday. (learn)
5 Our teacher ...... her birthday last week. (celebrate)

4 Look at the information and answer the questions.

True or false?

Mike washed his hair on Friday.

True.

Linda and Darren watched TV on Friday.

False. They played tennis on Friday.

1 Mike played football on Saturday.
2 Sue played tennis on Saturday.
3 Linda and Darren watched TV on Saturday.
4 Linda and Darren played football on Friday.
5 Mike played tennis on Sunday.

5 Write true sentences.

Mike / Sun

Mike watched TV on Sunday.

1 Mike / Sat
2 Sue / Fri
3 Linda and Darren / Sun
4 Sue / Sat
5 Linda and Darren / Fri

6 What about you and your family and friends? Write true sentences.

1 I ...... on Thursday.
2 My friends ...... on Saturday.
3 My family ...... on Sunday.
4 My brother / sister ...... on Wednesday.
5 I ...... on Friday.

Study skills

7 **Read the biography, the headings and the notes.**

BIOGRAPHY

MAHATMA GANDHI was born in 1869 in South Africa, but his nationality was Indian. He was a great political leader. He believed in non-violence. He wanted his country, India, to be independent and his struggle for independence from the British government was successful. His non-violent campaign defeated the British. Gandhi died in 1948. An assassin killed him. It was a tragic death for a very great man.

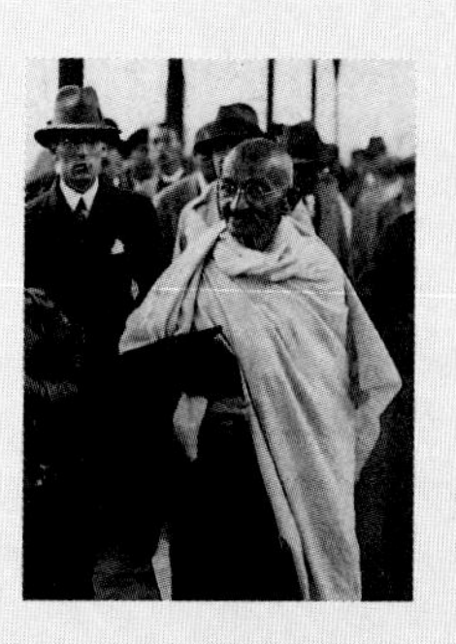

Headings	Notes
Name	Mahatma Gandhi
Dates	b. 1869 d. 1948
Nationality	Indian
Work	Politics: non-violence
Achievement	successful struggle for independence

8 **Use the same headings to make notes about this famous person.**

BIOGRAPHY

MARIE SKLODOWSKA was born in 1867, in Poland. She married Professor Pierre Curie, who was a Frenchman. So Marie Curie was Polish and French. She lived and worked in Paris. She was a great scientist. She discovered the chemical element, radium, and she helped to discover X-rays. She was a Nobel Prize winner twice: in 1903, for physics and, in 1911, for chemistry. She died in 1934.

Headings	Notes
Name	......
Dates	b. ...... d. ......
Nationality	......
Work	......
Achievement	......

9 **Revise the English vowels. Look, listen and repeat.** 3

1 long /iː/
These three trees

2 short /ɪ/
Thin little biscuits

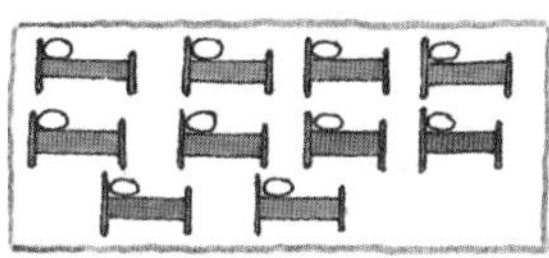
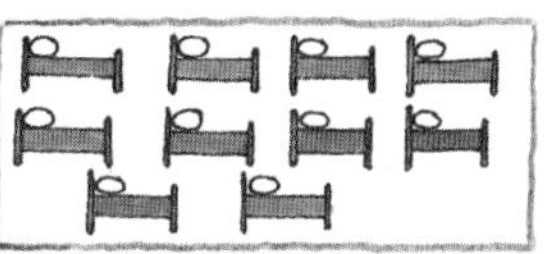

3 short /e/
Ten red beds

4 short /æ/
That bad cat

5 long /ɑː/
Mark's large car

6 short /ɒ/
Ron's got a lot

7 long /ɔː/
Paul's four daughters

8 short /ʊ/
Look at the cook

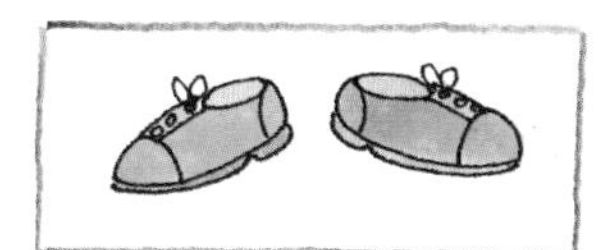

9 long /uː/
Two blue shoes

10 short /ʌ/
Mum's uncle

11 long /ɜː/
Dirty shirts

12 weak /ə/
Brother and sister

12c Vocabulary

Past, present and future

1 **Complete the table with the correct days, months and years.**

2 **Make a similar table in your notebook. Complete the chart with true information about the day, month and year *now*.**

the past		*the present*	*the future*	
the day before yesterday (1)	yesterday (2)	**today** (3) Saturday	tomorrow (4) Sunday	the day after tomorrow (5) ......
the month before last (6)	last month (7) July	**this month** (8) August	next month (9)	the month after next (10) ......
the year before last (11)	last year (12)	**this year** (13) 1998	next year (14)	the year after next (15) ......

3 **The Flames are a new pop group from Russia. Name the first six cities they visited on their world tour. Write the names of the cities and the dates.** 🎧4

1 London 1 June
2 ....
3 ....
4 ....
5 ....
6 ....

English across the curriculum

Language awareness

1 **Read the text.**

English in the modern world

In the reign of Queen Elizabeth I (1558–1603) there were only six million speakers of English. Most of them lived in Great Britain. But today, in the reign of her descendant, Queen Elizabeth II (1952–), there are many more speakers of English. And most of them do not live in Great Britain!

Three hundred million people speak English as their native language. English is their ***first*** language. They live in countries such as Britain, The United States of America, Canada, Australia and New Zealand.

Six hundred million people use English as an official, ***second*** language. They live in countries such as India, Pakistan and Nigeria.

But at least one hundred million people now study English as a ***foreign*** language. They live in countries such as Spain, Greece, Portugal, Mexico, Brazil, Argentina, China, Russia, Poland – in fact, almost everywhere.

Therefore, at least one thousand million people can read, speak, write and understand English today.

English is now an international language. In the modern world, people need English for work and for international communication. You can use English to help you meet new people and to make new friends in every country of the world.

2 **Complete the chart with the correct numbers. Use**

1,000,000,000 100,000,000 300,000,000 600,000,000

The number of people who speak English as a *first* language		......
The number of people who use English as a *second* language		......
The number of people who study English as a *foreign* language	at least	......
Total	at least	......

12d Skills work

Listening

1 Listen to these two young people. Choose the correct answers. 5

Ivan

1 Ivan was born in
   - **a)** Russia
   - **b)** Hungary
   - **c)** The USA

2 His native language is
   - **a)** Russian
   - **b)** Hungarian
   - **c)** English

3 He can speak
   - **a)** two languages
   - **b)** three languages
   - **c)** four languages

4 He thinks English is important because
   - **a)** it is necessary for business
   - **b)** it is necessary for foreign travel
   - **c)** it helps international communication

Yung Chang

1 Yung Chang was born in
   - **a)** Hong Kong
   - **b)** China
   - **c)** England

2 Her native language is
   - **a)** English
   - **b)** Mandarin Chinese
   - **c)** Cantonese Chinese

3 She can speak
   - **a)** one language
   - **b)** two languages
   - **c)** three languages

4 She thinks English is important because
   - **a)** it helps you get a job
   - **b)** it is useful on holidays abroad
   - **c)** it is an international language

Writing

2 Answer the questions about yourself. Write notes only.

1 Where were you born?
2 What is your native language?
3 How many languages can you speak?
4 Why do you think English is important?

3 Now change your notes in exercise 2 into sentences. Write a short paragraph about yourself.

I was born in ......

Speaking

4 Imagine you are another person from another country! Make notes about yourself, and then tell the class.

What's your name?
age?
date of birth?
first language?
reason for learning English?
You choose!

??????????????

Did you know?

In 1550, there were only 100,000 words in English.

Today, there are at least 750,000! How many English words do you know?

Progress Diary 12

Grammar

1 Write the past simple tense of these verbs.

play	played	learn	……
like	……	visit	……
dance	……		

Vocabulary

2 Look at the date, then answer the questions.

It's Saturday, 30 October.

What was the date the day before yesterday?

What's the date the day after tomorrow?

Communication

3 Write true sentences about the past.

wash my hair
I washed my hair last Thursday.
watch TV
play tennis, football, …
visit my uncle

4 Write the questions for these answers.

I'm fifteen.
Greek, English and some Spanish.
Yes, I'd love to dance.
No, it isn't my first trip.

Pronunciation

5 Practise English intonation.

English is easy! ↘ Is English easy? ↗

My progress

In unit 12 I like …… I don't like ……

He's got …

Listen and complete the words of the song. 6

He's got the whole ……, in his hands
He's got the whole wide ……, in his hands
He's got the whole ……, in his hands
He's got the whole …… in his hands.

He's got ……, in his hands
He's got ……, in his hands
He's got ……, in his hands
He's got the whole …… in his hands.

He's got ……, in his hands
He's got ……, in his hands
He's got ……, in his hands
He's got the whole …… in his hands.

the gym

the entrance hall

the office

a classroom

1 **Name the different rooms in your school.**

2 **Divide into groups. Each group is going to do a project about their ideal classroom.**

3 **In groups, draw a picture of your room. Label things in the room.**

4 **Now write a description of your ideal classroom.**

In our ideal classroom, there are sixteen chairs and three tables. There is a television ...

PROJECT

2 Our families

1 **Bring some photos of your family to the class.**

2 **In groups, ask and answer about your family photos.**

Are these your grandparents?

Yes, they are.

Who's this?

It's my uncle.

Is she your cousin?

No, she isn't. She's my aunt!

3 **Draw your family tree. Include ten to fifteen people, and their names.**

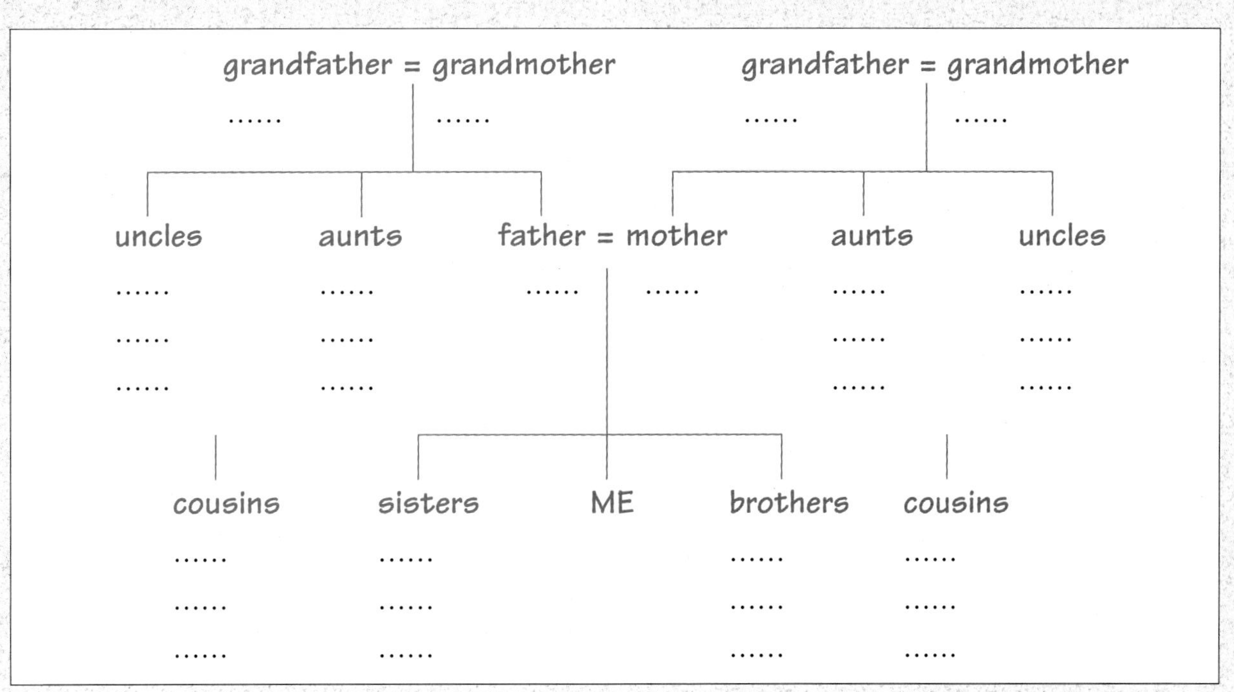

4 **Write a description of the people in your family tree.**

In my family, there are nine adults and six children. There are five men and four women. The five men are my two grandfathers, my two uncles, and my father. My grandfathers are called ...

Make posters to put on the wall.

1 **Copy the questionnaire into your notebook.**

	STUDENT 1	STUDENT 2	STUDENT 3
	......	......	......
1 What is your favourite animal?	......	......	......
2 Where does it live?	......	......	......
3 What does it eat?	......	......	......
4 What colour is it?	......	......	......
5 Is it in danger?			

2 **Now ask three students about their favourite animals. Write their answers in your notebook.**

3 **Write a paragraph about other peoples' favourite animals.**

There are three people in my questionnaire. Their names are Maria, Jan and Paul. Maria's favourite animal is a panda. It lives in China and eats bamboo. It is ...

Animals in danger

4 **Divide into groups. Each group is going to make a poster about animals in danger. In your poster, include:**

a slogan
a photograph or drawing

Display your posters in the school.

PROJECT

4 The environment

1 **Look at the pictures. Where do you think they are?**

2 **Divide into groups. Each group is going to do a project about one of the places in the pictures.**

3 **Collect material about your topic, for example, photos and newspaper articles in your language or in English.**

4 **In your group, write a short article about your topic. Include other material, for example, maps, photos, and advertisements.**

Kyoto

There are many old temples in Kyoto and tourism is an important industry.
There is a famous castle and the Emperor's palace. It is very beautiful.
There is a large factory near Kyoto. It makes

PROJECT

5 Our favourite pop stars

1 **Who is your favourite singer or group?**

2 **Find other students who have the same favourite singer or group.**

3 **Collect photos and magazine articles. In pairs or groups, make notes about your favourite singer or group.**

Our favourite singer is American.

Our favourite group is from Belfast.

4 **Write a short article about your favourite singer or group. Use the information in your notes.**

Bruce Springsteen is our favourite singer. He is from America. His

OUR FAVOURITE SINGER	
Name	......
Nationality	......
Age	......
Clothes	......
Best song	......

OUR FAVOURITE GROUP	
Names	......
Nationalities	......
Age	......
Clothes	......
Best song	......

Famous men and women from our country

1. List some famous men and women in your country's history.
2. Divide into groups. Each group is going to do a project about a famous man or woman in your country's history.
3. Make headings and notes about your famous person.

Name	......
Dates	......
Nationality	......
Work	......
Achievement	......
You choose!	......

4. Write a biography of your famous person. Include drawings, photos, quotations, and other useful information.

A BIOGRAPHY OF QUEEN VICTORIA

Main events in her life

Queen Victoria was born in 1819 in London, England. She was queen from 1837 to 1901. She married Albert in 1840 and they had nine children. She died in 1901.

Main achievements

Queen Victoria was queen for sixty-five years.

The Mystery of the Castle Diamonds

8
It is half past seven. Lady Castle, Inspector Shoelock Homes and his faithful assistant Dr. Witless are in the garden.
9
My diamonds! Where are my 24 beautiful diamonds? And my husband, Lord Castle, where is he?
Who's that? Who are you? Witless! Lady Castle! Quick! The music room!
PPST! The music room!
10
Ah! There's a message on the mirror. What does it say, Witless?
I don't know Inspector.
11
Have you got a mirror? What does it say?
How many diamonds are there:
in the piano ?
in the drum ?
in the trumpet ?
How many diamonds are there in the instruments?
In the violin? ..5..
In the trumpet? .....
In the drum? .....
In the guitar? .....
In the piano? .....
12
Just then ...
Who are you?
I am Lord Castle. I am Lady Castle's husband. And those are my diamonds!
No they aren't. They're MY diamonds. And we only have 23! Where's the 24th diamond? Where's the large famous Castle diamond?
Heh! Heh!

Answer the questions about *The Mystery of the Castle Diamonds*

1 **Who says:** 'Psst! The music room!'

Who is this person?

2 **Answer the questions in your notebook.**

1 What time does Lady Castle have a horrible surprise?

2 When does Inspector Homes arrive at Lady Castle's house?

3 What is the answer to clue number one?

4 What is the answer to clue number two?

5 Where does Inspector Homes see the message on the mirror?

6 What is the message in the mirror?

7 What is the **total** number of diamonds?

8 How many diamonds are there

in the piano?

in the drum?

in the trumpet?

in the guitar?

in the violin?

9 How many of the Castle diamonds does Inspector Homes find in the music room?

10 Where is the large, famous Castle diamond?

3 **Write the events of the story in their correct order.**

Correct order	Events
1	g Lady Castle loses her diamonds.
2	d Lady Castle phones the police.
3	……
4	……
5	……
6	……
7	……
8	……

a) Inspector Homes goes into the music room.

b) Inspector Homes finds clues 1 and 2.

c) We see Lord Castle!

d) Lady Castle phones the police.

e) Inspector Homes arrives at Lady Castle's house.

f) Inspector Homes sees the message on the mirror.

g) Lady Castle loses her diamonds.

h) Inspector Homes goes into the garden.

Sheila and the Toy Thieves

2

THX PLXN
DXTX: TXXSDXY
TWXNTY THXRD
DXCXMBER
TXMX: HXLF PXST TWX
XN THX MXRNING
PLXCX: MXNTY'S TXY
SHXP PXCCXDXLLY
LXNDXN
LOOK! The plan! Tuesday the twenty-third of December. Half past two in the morning. Monty's Toy Shop, Piccadilly, London,
What are they going to do Sheila?
They're going to steal all the Christmas toys! But we're going to tell the police!
AT THE POLICE STATION
Ha! Ha! A computer plan? But thieves don't understand computers. And little girls don't understand them! It's a mistake. Go home and play with your toy computer!
What are you going to do?
I'm going to give the thieves another plan! Watch!
Oh, the police are stupid!
IN ANOTHER PART OF LONDON
Look! Our computer is changing the plan! But it isn't giving capital letters or spaces
importantthepolicearegoingtobeat
montysshop
thenewplan
changedatefrom23rddecemberto22nd
decemberchangetimefromhalfpasttwo
toquartertofourchangeplacefrommonty's
toyshoppiccadillytoharrodstoyshop
knightsbridge
WHAT IS 'THEIR' NEW PLAN? : Date ... Time ... Place ...

THE NEW PLAN
DATE: 22nd Dec
TIME: 3.45 a.m
PLACE: Harrods Toy Shop Knightsbridge
SHEILA, MIKE AND THE MANAGERESS ARE IN THE TOY DEPARTMENT
I'm going to be Superman!
And I'm going to phone the police!
I'm going to be the gorilla!
NO! Don't phone them! They don't believe us!
You're going to be Donald Duck!
Donald Duck? Me! Well, OK.
NOW THEY'RE HIDING. THEY'RE WAITING ...
SUDDENLY
Ha! We've got you!
Who are you!
I'm your computer operator.
The new computer plan! You! No!
LATER ... SHEILA MEETS A VERY SPECIAL PERSON AT BUCKINGHAM PALACE ...
SHEILA BRIGGS
Computer Genius saves Christmas toys
A VERY CLEVER GIRL
QUEEN
For Sheila Briggs, this gold medal and a new computer.
For the police, nothing!
THE END

Answer these questions about *Sheila and the Toy Thieves*

1 **Copy and complete the table in your notebook.**

Put the events of the story into their correct order.

Correct order	Events
1	e
2	h
3	......
4	......
5	......
6	......
7	......
8	......

a) Sheila catches the criminals.

b) Sheila sends the criminals a new plan.

c) Sheila goes to Harrod's Toy Shop.

d) Sheila hides and waits for the criminals.

e) Sheila receives a computer for her birthday.

f) Sheila gets a gold medal from the Queen.

g) Sheila talks to the police about the criminals' plan.

h) Sheila's computer shows a plan by some criminals.

i) The police do not believe Sheila's story.

1 e Sheila receives a computer for her birthday.

2 h Sheila's computer shows a plan by some criminals.

2 **Copy and complete the two plans in your notebook.**

Plan 1

The criminals' original plan

shop	Monty's Toy Shop
address	......
day	......
date	......
time	......

Plan 2

Sheila's new plan for the criminals

shop	......
address	......
day	......
date	......
time	......

3 **Here is a special message for you. What is the message? Who is it from?**

CXNGRXTXLXTXXNS!

YXX XRX MXKXNG GXXD PRXGRXSS.

GXXD LXCK WXTH YXXR XNGLXSH.

THX QXXXN

Grammar Summary

Verbs

present simple: *be*

affirmative		**negative**		**interrogative**	**short answers**	
short forms	*full forms*	*short forms*	*full forms*			
I'm	I am	I'm not	I am not	Am I …?	Yes, I am.	No, I'm not.
you're	you are	you aren't	you are not	Are you …?	Yes, you are.	No, you aren't.
she he 's it	she he is it	she he isn't it	she he is not it	she Is he …? it	she Yes, he is. it	she No, he isn't. it
we you 're they	we you are they	we you aren't they	we you are not they	we Are you …? they	we Yes, you are. they	we No, you aren't. they

Examples

I'm from Wales. They aren't students.
He is fourteen. Are you from Australia?

Contractions are short forms. We use contractions when we speak and when we write informal letters to friends. We use full forms when we write formal letters.

present simple: regular verbs

affirmative	**negative**	**interrogative**	**short answers**	
I you like	I you don't like	Do I you like …?	Yes, I you do.	No, I you don't.
she he likes it	she he doesn't like it	she Does he like …? it	she Yes, he does. it	she No, he doesn't. it
we you like they	we you don't like they	we Do you like …? they	we Yes, you do. they	we No, you don't. they

don't = do not doesn't = does not

Examples

We swim at school. They don't drink beer.
He watches TV every day. Do you eat pizza?
She doesn't like tennis.

We use the present simple to talk about regular routines and hobbies.

present simple: *have got*

affirmative	negative	interrogative	short answers	
I you 've got	I you haven't got	Have I you got ...?	Yes, I you have.	No, I you haven't.
she he 's got it	she he hasn't got it	she Has he got ...? it	she Yes, he has. it	she No, he hasn't. it
we you 've got they	we you haven't got they	we Have you got ...? they	we Yes, you have. they	we No, you haven't. they

've got = have got   's got = has got

Examples

I've got two sisters.   He hasn't got a red scarf.   Have you got a dog?

*We use **have got** to talk about possessions and relationships.*

present continuous

affirmative	negative	interrogative	short answers	
I'm playing	I'm not playing	Am I playing?	Yes, I am.	No, I'm not.
you're playing	you aren't playing	Are you playing?	Yes, you are.	No, you're not.
she he 's playing it	she he isn't playing it	she Is he playing? it	she Yes, he is. it	she No, he isn't. it
we you 're playing they	we you aren't playing they	we Are you playing? they	we Yes, you are. they	we No, you 're not. they

We use the present continuous to talk about actions in the present.
We can also use the present continuous to talk about the future.

Compare the two meanings of the present continuous

Meaning A

*It is used to talk about actions **in the present**.*

Linda is playing tennis at the moment.
Darren is watching her.

Meaning B

*It is used to talk about actions **in the future**.*

Sue is staying at home tomorrow, she isn't going to school.
Mike is buying a new bike next Saturday.

*We also use **going to** to talk about the future.*

Examples

I'm going to play basketball tonight.
He isn't going to see the film next weekend.
Are you going to Portugal next month? Yes, we are.

past simple: *be*

affirmative	negative	interrogative	short answers	
I was	I wasn't	Was I …?	Yes, I was.	No, I wasn't.
you were	you weren't	Were you …?	Yes, you were.	No, you weren't.
she he was it	she he wasn't it	she Was he …? it	she Yes, he was. it	she No, he wasn't. it
we you were they	we you weren't they	we Were you …? they	we Yes, you were. they	we No, you weren't. they

Examples
I was in Japan last year.
She wasn't at school yesterday.
Were they in London last Tuesday?

past simple: regular verbs

base form	past simple
learn	learn**ed**
visit	visit**ed**
walk	walk**ed**
rain	rain**ed**
like	like**d**
love	love**d**
start	start**ed**

Examples
I learned French at school.
He walked to the sports centre.
It rained all day yesterday.
We loved the film.

We use the past simple to talk about actions in the past.

present simple: *can*

affirmative	negative	interrogative	short answers	
I you she he can it we you they	I you she he cannot/can't it we you they	I you she Can he ...? it we you they	I you she Yes, he can. it we you they	I you she No, he can't. it we you they

*We use **can** to talk about ability and permission.*

Examples

Ability
She can swim two kilometres.

Permission
Steve Mum can I have an ice-cream?
Mum Yes, you can, but you can't have a coke.

present simple: *must*

affirmative	negative	interrogative	short answers	
I you she he must it we you they	I you she he mustn't it we you they	I you she Must he ...? it we you they	I you she Yes, he must. it we you they	I you she No, he mustn't. it we you they

Examples
I must finish my work.
She mustn't play tennis.
Must we go to bed?

*We use **must** to talk about obligation.*
*There is no past tense of **must**.*

Note *The third person singular (she/he/it) in the verbs **must** and **can** do not change.*

Imperatives

	affirmative	negative
be	Be quiet!	Don't be stupid!
all other verbs	Follow me!	Don't forget the tickets!

We use imperatives to tell people what to do and give instructions.

Articles

a table **an** umbrella
the boy **the** apple

*Use **a** before consonants:* a boy, a town.
*Use **an** before a vowel sound:* an apple, an egg.
***a / an** are not used with plurals or uncountable nouns.*

Plurals: regular nouns

group 1		group 2	
singular	*plural*	*singular*	*plural*
door	door**s**	bus	bus**es**
map	map**s**	sandwich	sandwich**es**
girl	girl**s**		
boy	boy**s**		

Countable and uncountable nouns

countable		uncountable
singular	*plural*	*singular only*
tomato	tomato**es**	cheese
orange	orange**s**	tea
sandwich	sandwich**es**	soup

Countable nouns can be both singular and plural.

Examples

a tomato two tomatoes
an orange six oranges

Uncountable nouns have no plural form.

some* and *any

*We use **some** and **any** before uncountable and plural countable nouns when we want to talk about an indefinite quantity or number.*

Examples

countable nouns	
affirmative	There are **some** hamburgers.
negative	There aren't **any** books.
interrogative	Are there **any** apples?

uncountable nouns	
affirmative	There's **some** cheese.
negative	There isn't **any** tea.
interrogative	Is there **any** coffee?

Pronouns and adjectives

	personal pronouns		possessive adjectives
	subject	*object*	
singular	I	me	my
	you	you	your
	she	her	her
	he	him	his
	it	it	its
plural	we	us	our
	you	you	your
	they	them	their

Examples
That's my book. Give it to me.
We've got a rabbit. Its name is Snowy.
Our sports teacher is great. He teaches us tennis.

Prepositions

of place

in England
in the south
in the bedroom
in the garden
in the shower

at home
at school

on the table
on the desk
on the stairs
on the roof

of time

in the morning(s)
in the afternoon(s)
in the evening(s)
in April
in the spring

at the weekend
at ten o'clock

on Saturday(s)
on Tuesday morning
on 22 May

Examples
The party is **on** Friday.
The party is **on** 21 June.
The party is **in** June.

Conjunctions

Spain **and** Greece are in Europe.
Canada is in North America, **but** Brazil is in South America.

Acknowledgements

Design by Holdsworth Associates

Story page illustrations by Wendy Cantor

Story page photography by Stephen Oliver

Illustrations by
Paul Burnell, Wendy Cantor, Antonia Enthoven/The Garden Studio, Alison Everitt, Rosamund Fowler, Anthony Godber, Neil Hague/Route 69, Lorraine Harrison, Michael Hill, Conny Jude, Maggie Ling, Frances Lloyd, Mac Macintosh, Fiona MacVicar/The Inkshed, Stephen May, Colin Mier, Mike Nicholson, Francis Scappaticci/Maggie Mundy, Susan Scott, Martin Shovel, Hannah Stuart, Technical Graphics Dept (OUP), Raymond Turvey, Russell Walker, Lis Watkins/Pennant Agency, David Williams

Photography by Rob Judges, Garry O'Brien and Stephen Oliver

The publishers would like to thank the following for permission to reproduce photographs
Action-Plus, Allsport UK Ltd, James Davis Travel Photography, The Environmental Picture Library, Mary Evans Picture Library, Fortean Picture Library, Greenpeace Communications Ltd, Robert Harding Picture Library, Hulton Deutsch Collection Ltd, The Image Bank, Oxford Scientific Films Ltd, Retna Pictures Ltd, Rex Features Ltd, Sygma, Tropix Photographic Library, John Walmsley Photo-Library, Zefa Picture Library (UK) Ltd

Story page models supplied by
Catwalk Show Productions, Lilliput Model Agency, Sparkle Stage Set

The publishers would like to thank the following for their time and assistance
Boswell H. & Co. Ltd (Oxford), Cambridge Tourist Information, Carters Supermarket (Faringdon), Cheney School (Oxford), Elmer Cotton Sports (Oxford), London Buses Ltd, Martins Newsagent (Carterton), Pet World (Oxford), St Barnabas School (Oxford)

The publishers would like to thank the following for their comments on the manuscript of *Open Doors*
Sandie Allen, Norberto Cerezal, Marisa Constantanides, John Field, José Ramón Insa, Jack Jennison, Rosa López Boullón, Mike Macfarlane, Mike McGrath, Kevin McNicholas, Miguel Murcia, Mª Cristina Riera, Jo von Waskowski, Kate Wakeman, Ann Ward

This book is dedicated to the memory of Christopher John Whitney

Oxford University Press
Walton Street, Oxford OX2 6DP

Oxford New York Toronto Madrid Delhi Bombay Calcutta Madras Karachi Kuala Lumpur Singapore Hong Kong Tokyo Nairobi Dar es Salaam Cape Town Melbourne Auckland
and associated companies in
Berlin Ibadan

OXFORD and OXFORD ENGLISH are trade marks of Oxford University Press

ISBN 0 19 435600 0

First published 1994

Printed in Spain by Mateu Cromo, S.A. Pinto (Madrid)